Commanding an Air Force Squadron in the Twenty-First Century

A Practical Guide of Tips and Techniques for Today's Squadron Commander

JEFFRY F. SMITH
Lieutenant Colonel, USAF

Air University Press
Maxwell Air Force Base, Alabama

August 2003

Air University Library Cataloging Data

Smith, Jeffry F.
    Commanding an Air Force squadron in the twenty-first century : a practical guide of tips and techniques for today's squadron commander / Jeffry F. Smith.
        p. ; cm.
    Includes bibliographical references and index.
    Contents: Critical months -- The mission -- People -- Communicative leadership -- The good, the bad and the ugly -- Cats and dogs -- Your exit strategy.
    ISBN 1-58566-119-8
    1. United States. Air Force -- Officers' handbooks. 2. Command of troops. I. Title.
    358.4/1330/41—dc21

Disclaimer

Opinions, conclusions, and recommendations expressed or implied are solely those of the author and do not necessarily represent the views of Air University, the United States Air Force, the Department of Defense, or any other US government agency. Cleared for public release: distribution unlimited.

Air University Press
131 West Shumacher Avenue
Maxwell AFB AL 36112–6615
http://aupress.maxwell.af.mil

To my parents, Carl and Marty Smith,
whose example of truth, ethics, and integrity
shaped my life. And to my wife Cheryl and sons
Stephen and Andrew, whose love, support, and service to
our Air Force has been my inspiration to continue to serve.

Contents

Foreword

The opportunity to command is a tremendous honor and responsibility and unquestionably will be one of the most significant roles of your Air Force career. The very nature of command is unique to the military; there is no civilian equivalent for this level of trust, authority, and responsibility. The essence of command is leadership, and your example will set the standard for your entire organization. For this reason, command is reserved for those individuals exhibiting only the highest levels of integrity, selflessness, and excellence.

Leadership is not accomplished from behind the desk or by way of E-mail; rather, effective leadership requires you to lead from out front. Since the responsibilities of such leadership may appear daunting to first-time commanders, our Air Force places significant emphasis on precommand training to ensure your readiness for these new responsibilities. Immerse yourself in the available training to ensure you fully understand the rules of engagement.

There is much to learn from the insights, experiences, and recommendations of previous commanders. Lt Col Jeff Smith's *Commanding an Air Force Squadron in the Twenty-First Century* provides some excellent perspectives from current and graduated commanders to help set your course and prepare you for the best job in the Air Force.

Congratulations on your command and Godspeed!

JOHN P. JUMPER
General, USAF
Chief of Staff

About the
Author

Lt Col Jeffry F. Smith was born on 22 January 1961 in Roswell, New Mexico. After graduating from Bishop Ireton High School in Alexandria, Virginia, he entered the Pennsylvania State University on a four-year Reserve Officer Training Corps academic scholarship. He obtained a Bachelor of Arts degree in Political Science and International Affairs in 1983. He has a master's degree in Management from Embry-Riddle Aeronautical University and a similar degree in Strategic Studies from Air University, Maxwell AFB, Alabama. Colonel Smith completed resident courses in Squadron Officer School in 1987, Air Command and Staff College in 1994, Armed Forces Staff College in 1995, and Air War College in 2002.

Colonel Smith entered active duty at Williams AFB, Arizona, in August 1983. He graduated from Undergraduate Pilot Training in August 1984 and entered B-52G Combat Crew Training at Castle AFB, California, where he was a distinguished graduate. His first assignment was to the 441st Bomb Squadron at Mather AFB, California, where he performed co-pilot and evaluator co-pilot duties. In 1988 Colonel Smith was board-selected to attend B-1B training at Dyess AFB, Texas. An outstanding graduate of both B-1B initial qualification training and pilot upgrade training and a distinguished graduate of the Central Flight Instructor Course, he was assigned to Grand Forks AFB, North Dakota. He served with the 46th Bomb Squadron as pilot, evaluator pilot, aircraft commander, instructor pilot, and squadron training flight instructor pilot. He holds three B-1B time-to-climb world records.

In March 1992 Colonel Smith was assigned to Headquarters Eighth Air Force as aide-de-camp and then executive officer to the commander. In July 1993 he attended Air Command and Staff College at Maxwell AFB, Alabama. Upon graduation, he was assigned as operations officer, Operations Directorate (J37); and as Joint Task Force training action officer (J38), Headquarters USCINCPAC, Camp H. M. Smith, Hawaii. During his tour at Pacific Command, he attended Armed Forces Staff College and Joint Professional Military Education Phase II and was subsequently selected as a joint specialty officer. In May 1996 he was reassigned to the 9th Bomb Squadron, Dyess AFB, Texas, as assistant director of operations. He was then selected as deputy commander, 7th Operations Support Squadron in September 1997.

Colonel Smith took command of the 37th Bomb Squadron at Ellsworth AFB, South Dakota, in July 1999. He led the 28th Bomb Wing's largest combat flying squadron of more than 490 personnel assigned and 13 B-1B aircraft valued at more than $3.6 billion. In July 2001, he was selected to attend the Air War College at Maxwell AFB, Alabama, for the academic year 2002.

Colonel Smith's decorations include the Defense Meritorious Service Medal, Meritorious Service Medal (with three oak leaf clusters), Air Medal, Aerial Achievement Medal, Air Force Commendation Medal, Joint Service Achievement Medal, Air Force Achievement Medal, Combat Readiness Medal (with two oak leaf clusters), National Defense Service Medal, and Humanitarian Service Medal.

He is a command pilot with more than 3,100 hours in the T-37, T-38, B-52G, and B-1B aircraft. Colonel Smith and his wife, the former Cheryl Vanderpool of Los Angeles, California, have two sons, Stephen and Andrew.

Preface

Col Timothy T. Timmons was the original author of the book entitled, *Commanding an Air Force Squadron*. He wrote it while he was a student at the National War College in 1989. The staff of the National Defense University supported his research, and Air University Press published the original book in 1993.

I had the privilege of reading his book for the first time while I was a student at Air Command and Staff College. I loved it. I found it extremely useful, insightful, and full of pertinent stories from officers who had just left command. I then reread it in 1999 when I was selected to command the 37th Bomb Squadron "Tigers," a large B-1 flying squadron at Ellsworth AFB, South Dakota. While I found many of his basic command principles timeless, I also realized that much of the United States Air Force had changed in the last decade or so, and his wonderful work was in need of an update to reflect command in the twenty-first century. I thought it would be a shame if someone didn't take the opportunity to rewrite his book.

My opportunity came when I was selected to attend Air War College. The commandant at the time was Maj Gen David MacGhee, who, in his welcoming and opening remarks, issued a challenge to the students: "Make a difference while you're here." *Commanding an Air Force Squadron in the Twenty-First Century* is my attempt to make a difference.

Because Timmons's original work was so excellent and familiar to a generation of United States Air Force officers, I decided to write a new book, using his original framework, reflecting the changes of the Air Force since its original production. I believe this book captures those changes, and I hope the reader finds the work equally engaging, and that someone will take the baton to write the third edition when necessary.

This book won't depart much from the original framework for a very good reason—"don't mess with something that's good"—advice that I heeded many times while I was in command. Because of the demographic diversity of squadrons today, I've made every attempt to broaden the base of the original book to ensure this effort covers a wide and balanced range of commanders' experiences.

Let me tell you what this book is *not* about, and perhaps that will shed some light on what it *is* about. It is not full of checklists. Don't flip to a chapter dealing with discipline, death, or how to build unit cohesion looking for a simple, cookbook approach to the problem. You'll be disappointed. It takes leadership to make those things happen.

This book is not a scholarly effort—nor is it intended to be. In fact, it is an "easy read" for those who are about to assume the intense responsibility of command. This book does not espouse particular leadership or command duties and responsibilities. There are many excellent readings by very talented and more qualified people on those subjects.

Commanding an Air Force Squadron in the Twenty-First Century is about commanders—those that have recently come from exciting commands across the entire Air Force. I interviewed more than 100 airmen—mostly commanders who just completed tours at the helm of their squadron on the recent successes, and failures, of their commands—to provide you, the incoming squadron commander, a collection of experiences you can relate to when the situation arises on your watch.

This book's advice may not meet every reader's needs because the size and demographics of Air Force squadrons today vary significantly. As you will discover, there are nearly as many different types of squadrons as there are commanders. Some had small squadrons (25–75 personnel) and some had large squadrons (400–600). Some had detached units (recruiting squadrons), and some had traditional home-based units (maintenance squadrons). Some had squadrons that experienced heavy Operations Tempo issues (flying squadrons), while others commanded traditional in-garrison units with their own unique challenges (medical squadrons). Each commander dealt with specific issues unique to his or her squadron, and many faced common challenges. Capturing the most valuable of these experiences on paper is the objective of this work.

Although this book contains many examples of successes these commanders enjoyed throughout their tenure, it also highlights mistakes they made. I was tremendously impressed with their acknowledgement of failure and their willingness to share the lessons learned with me to pass on to future commanders. Their selfless generosity was exceptional and greatly appreciated.

One common critique made by almost every officer interviewed was that although most of our Air Force's major commands now have a formal course for soon-to-be squadron commanders, they are often too short and too broad to handle many of the issues you'll face as a commander. Understandably, these courses cannot teach you how to cook because there's no recipe for the countless different issues you may face. They do not, and arguably cannot, touch every subject.

Until you've had to accompany the Department of Social Services case worker to take a child from one of your troops' homes, spend hours in the community hospital's "grieving" room upon the death of one of your personnel, spend part of Thanksgiving visiting one of your members in jail, or make a tough call that negatively impacts a friend's career, you can't truly comprehend the infinite dilemmas inherent with such responsibility. This book touches on the realities of squadron command today by providing a few examples to which you can refer when the "similar" situation arises. Remember, it is neither a textbook nor a checklist. Rather, it is one of the many tools you will place in a very large toolbox for building a successful command.

Leadership is the most studied but least understood of the social sciences. Yet, it is leadership that you must have to successfully lead an Air Force squadron. Use this book, this tool, to help you think through some of the challenges that lie ahead. Enjoy.

Many thanks go to my fellow classmates at Air War College for offering their valuable time in support of my efforts. I appreciate the generous time these officers spent with me during interviews, but the ultimate thanks will come from those future commanders who learn from their experiences. Particularly, thanks go to Col Celeste Suminsby, Lt Cols Jay Carlson, Scott Hanson, Eileen Isola, Terry Kono, and Robert Suminsby, and Maj Scott Merrell, who spent countless hours editing, advising, redirecting, and helping me focus on the right issues that capture life in squadron command today.

I also thank Dr. Richard Lester, dean of Academic Affairs at Air University's Center for Professional Development, for his assistance in helping me frame the book's content and his constant encouragement. I thank the faculty of Air War College for their complete support in my endeavors. Most importantly, I must thank my principal cheerleader and Air War College staff sponsor, Dr. Daniel Hughes. Without his insightful guidance, exceptional advice, and tremendous editing abilities, this work never would have happened. His experiences as an accomplished and widely published author helped me immensely in my efforts, and I am deeply and forever grateful.

Introduction

The concept of command in a military setting is nothing new. It proliferates throughout most good history books. Many different individuals have exercised this phenomenon called command: Alexander the Great as he conquered the known world; Attila the Hun in the fifth century A.D.; Generals Robert E. Lee and Ulysses S. Grant against each other during our Civil War; and General of the Army Dwight D. Eisenhower in Europe during the Second World War. These leaders are certainly a varied grouping: they were literally and figuratively worlds apart; they were surely loved by thousands of people and probably despised by an equal number, and, with the exception of Lee and Grant, lived in different eras. But they shared this one common thread—military command. You can find all five men in any encyclopedia, and history views them as famous individuals in part because of their success while they were in command.

In the United States Air Force, an officer's first opportunity to command in the true sense of the word occurs at the squadron level. Most Air Force officers who have been commanders will tell you that their command tours were the best years of their careers, and a majority of those who commanded at multiple levels will tell you that squadron command was the absolute pinnacle. Why is this the case? What's so great about squadron command? What's the big deal? People say it's unique. Why?

Consider the Air Force's military environment. If someone asks an Air Force member what he or she does for a living, the response usually is "I am in the Air Force." Ask someone you may meet in Detroit what they do for a living and he or she usually responds that he or she works for General Motors—the person will NOT tell you that they are "in" General Motors, just as the airman will NOT tell you that they "work for" the Air Force. Small words in a reply to a question, but those words carry a big meaning.

Next, consider the responsibility and power of a military commander. As a commander, you are responsible for your unit's mission, all of the unit's members, and all of their families. A military commander serves 24/7 and constantly lives in a fish-bowl. While exercising authority under the Uniform Code of Military Justice or other instructions and regulations, a commander can immediately demote an individual, jail the airman, and retrieve the airman in certain circumstances. The power of the chief executive officer of General Motors does not approximate the wide breadth of responsibility or depth of power of the military commander.

Finally, consider the Air Force squadron—where the rubber meets the road and the mission is actually performed. Squadron command is unique because it is the one point in an officer's career where the officer is very close to the mission and is in charge. Earlier positions may have been close to the mission, but someone else was in charge and later commands at higher levels are too far removed from the actual mission. These are three major factors why many officers, active and retired, will tell you his or her squadron command was the pinnacle of his or her career.

This book is all about squadron command. Colonel-select Jeff Smith has done a tremendous job in gathering the thoughts and ideas of many commanders, including himself, and offering the reader the opportunity to learn from literally a hundred former and current commanders. After conducting extensive research, Colonel Smith presents "the best of the best" on a wide range of topics that directly apply to squadron commanders.

Commanding an Air Force Squadron in the Twenty-First Century does not pretend to present the patented answer to any problem, issue, or situation. Colonel Smith does not direct you to read or study instructions and regulations as if you need textbook answers to command a squadron—you don't. Finally, he does not discuss units other than squadrons and does not discuss squadron command as if it were accomplished in the first 50 years of our Air Force's history.

What Colonel Smith does do is to present a plethora of accounts of how recent and current squadron commanders have approached today's situations, problems, and issues. He paints a picture of commanding a squadron through the eyes of a hundred individuals and offers it to the reader in a well-written, easy-to-read format that might be best described as

"Dutch uncle advice." Any commander or soon-to-be commander can pick up this book, read it in a relatively short time, and come away with new ideas or methods that he or she will be able to apply to his or her own situation.

This book is similar to a book I wrote 13 years ago on the same subject. My book was becoming outdated with each passing year. Times have changed: Air Force demographics have become much more diversified as have the demographics of commanders; the organization level of a group has been introduced; the concept of the Expeditionary Air Force has become day-to-day reality; and we have engaged in wars in the Middle East. Jeff's book is broader in scope, updated in time, and, quite honestly, an improvement of my work.

Besides presenting the views of today's Air Force officers, Colonel Smith introduces a few thoughts of such notable figures as General of the Air Force Henry H. "Hap" Arnold, Lt Col Joshua Chamberlain, Napoleon, Abraham Lincoln, and Aristotle at key points in the text to provide added meaning to the subject at hand. His text discussing the relationship between a commander and their first sergeant is particularly well written and critical to the well being of any unit. One of Jeff's chapters, "Cats and Dogs," touches on a few topics not often discussed in books on command but still important to any commander. Most importantly, this book focuses on the basics of squadron command and does so with a straightforward writing style.

Today's Air Force squadron commanders may not all be featured in the encyclopedia as the five men mentioned earlier, but they will share one thing in common with them—the unique experience that comes with military command. This book helps to make that experience better, easier, and more meaningful. Enjoy a very good book!

TIMOTHY T. TIMMONS
Colonel, USAF, Retired

Chapter 1

Critical Months

It is sometimes frustrating to try and explain to someone—military or civilian—what this "being a commander" thing is all about simply because they cannot possibly understand the depth, complexity, and hours involved. Nor could you. I am a teacher, counselor, rescuer, parent, mentor, confessor, judge and jury, executioner, cheerleader, coach, nudger, butt-kicker, hugger, social worker, lawyer, shrink, doctor, analyst, budgeteer, allowance giver, career planner, assignment getter, inspector, critiquer, scheduler, planner, shopper, social eventer, party thrower, and absolutely as often as possible— sacrificial lamb. I am my squadron's commander, and will only do this job one way while I'm in it . . . whatever it takes to serve them.

—Lt Col Eileen Isola, Commander
463d Operations Support Squadron

Introduction

Congratulations on your selection to command an Air Force squadron! Starting off on the right foot as a squadron commander is critical to the overall success of a command tour. Assuming this is your first opportunity to command, it would be helpful to hit the ground running when you take your squadron's guidon. This chapter discusses the critical period from the time you are officially notified of your selection to command a unit until you have been in command for about three months (or until the "honeymoon" is over). Experience has proven that a commander who is "ahead of the ballgame" during this period will stay ahead.

Before Taking Over

Certain moments in an officer's career stand out as unique or special. Receiving the news that you've been selected for command is certainly one such special moment. Most officers who have commanded an Air Force squadron will remember clearly where they were and how they received the news. The moment you learned of your selection will stand as a cherished memory.

Many commanders will also tell you how busy they became between the time of their selection for squadron command and the actual time of their change of command. If you thought you were busy before, imagine trying to close out your old job and diving into your new one—all at the same time!

Time management is critical during this period because you will be pulled in many different directions. The bottom line: you must establish your priorities between the responsibilities of your current position and gathering information about the new job. As the change of command approaches, it is wise to slowly phase out of the old job and devote more time to learning the new one.

One commander interviewed told of her selection for command while assigned to the Air Staff at the Pentagon. She had to prepare for a short-notice overseas permanent change of station (PCS) in addition to concluding some important Air Staff projects. Because of these circumstances, her last two months in the Pentagon were the busiest two months of her career—leaving her with little time to gather information about her upcoming command. The same may happen to you, so start preparing yourself now.

Many former squadron commanders were asked what actions they took before taking the reins of command. The consensus was that within the individual circumstances and time available, a new commander-designate should concentrate on the four following items in order of priority:

1. Understand the squadron's mission.
2. Learn the squadron's personnel.
3. Meet the chain of command.
4. Understand the role of other units on the base.

Lt Col Roderick Zastrow commanded the 44th Fighter Squadron (FS) (F-15C) at Kadena Air Base (AB) in Japan. He, too, thought it imperative to have a well-thought-out plan of attack before taking command. He believed an officer selected

2

Proverb for Command

Command is a special trust. The legal and moral responsibilities of commanders exceed those of any other leader of similar position or authority. Nowhere else does a boss have to answer for how subordinates live and what they do after work. Our society and the institution look to the commander to make sure that missions succeed, that the people receive the proper training and care, and that values survive. On the one hand, the nation grants commanders special authority to be good stewards of its most precious resources: freedom and people. On the other hand, those citizens serving in the Air Force also trust their commanders to lead them well. You will have the authority to set policy and punish misconduct. It's no wonder that organizations take on the personal stamp of their commander. Those selected to command offer something beyond their formal authority—their personal example and public actions have tremendous moral force. You alone are the one who must embody the commitment of the USAF to operational readiness and care of its people.[1]

---

for command needed to "develop a commander's mindset." He added, "Commanding appears pure and simple in theory, but becomes inexplicably complex in practice. Therefore, I strongly suggest that a command mind-set does not start at the change of command—or it should not if you and your boss can help it. Those with a goal to command, and those would-be detachment commanders or operations officers, need to have carefully thought through the ideals of command prior to formally assuming command."[2]

Much of your thought process of command responsibilities will have come from your experiences as a commander's subordinate. Personally, I have had good commanders and I've had better commanders. I learned something from each of them as I grew up under their leadership. Colonel Zastrow offered this tip: "As a starting point in developing a command framework, write down the good, the bad, and the ugly observations of former commanders. Keeping a separate, informal section of notes aside for the next level of officership—in this case squadron command—can serve as a constantly evolving lifelong reference. Take note of how commanders lead, their personalities, their plans, their personal management styles, their scheduling guidance, how they conducted meetings, how they rewarded, and how they disciplined."[3]

Lt Col Kurt Klausner had the benefit of three commands, one as an O-3 detachment commander, the second as an O-4 taking command of a combat communications squadron, and the third as an O-5 commander of the 53d Computer Systems Squadron (CSS), Eglin Air Force Base (AFB), Florida. He used the experiences from his first command to make sure he didn't repeat any earlier mistakes and took the opportunity to capitalize on his many successes. One lesson learned was to ensure his family was squared away before the day of his change of command. Although he was coming from a different base to take command of the 53d CSS, he smartly negotiated with both his losing and gaining group commanders to allow a few days to get his family moved into housing and household goods set up and to deal with the many "postmove" maladies that often accompany a short-notice PCS. "Once you take the guidon, you've got it. I didn't have to worry about taking care of my family at the very same time I faced my new squadron on the first day. It was a tremendous personal relief."[4]

Whether you are coming into a new base with a new wing environment or are already established in the wing in another job (such as director of operations or squadron deputy commander), many things will determine the amount of homework you need to do regarding your new assignment. If you've just "PCSed" inbound, get as much information as you can about the wing's mission, culture, and leadership prior to taking command. This background will give you a tremendous leg up on your first three months in the saddle. One good source of information for Colonel Klausner was his major air command functional officer. "I spoke with the ACC/SC about my new squadron. He provided a great insight from his strategic view of the squadron as to where we stood. He was free to give me an unbiased opinion and general advice even before I started. He raised several red flags that had my immediate interest and helped me focus my priorities."[5]

Studying and understanding the environment you are about to enter can be incredibly helpful to you and your unit. Understanding what pitfalls lie ahead and what specific challenges you are about to face will give you an opportunity to attack them accordingly. Col (then lieutenant colonel) Mark Browne had perhaps the greatest leadership challenge of command: taking a squadron that was down in morale and one that was ranked number 27 of 28 recruiting squadrons in the United States Air Force (USAF) Recruiting Command. He was responsible for multiple detached flights. He took command of the fledgling 348th Recruiting Squadron in the summer of 1998, a difficult time for Air Force recruiting efforts in general. In 1998 the USAF barely met its recruiting goals, and in 1999 it failed to meet its goal for the first time in history.

Colonel Browne attacked this significant leadership challenge directly. He spoke at length with the commander of Air Force recruiting and was given, in a period of nearly two hours, "the greatest one-way conversation about leadership and integrity I'd ever heard."[6] But be aware—not all one-way conversations are positive, and not all advice offered from the command staff level give the appropriate "in the trenches" perspective. Balancing strategic-level advice with your tactical-level reality is necessary. Under Colonel Browne's command, the squadron shot up in ratings and exceeded the extended active duty recruiting goal in 1999 for the first time in many years. His direct, hands-on, proactive leadership approach made the difference.

All commanders and former commanders interviewed agreed that it is best to make a clean break with your former job when taking on a new command—to finish all the taskings and paperwork associated with your old duty before the change of command. Once the change of command occurs, your new duty will demand 100 percent of your time.

Your departure from your old job may generate several officer and enlisted performance reports that need closure, all of which will need to be completed before you leave to take command. You also may have been heavily involved in working personnel issues on behalf of your commander. These, too, need to either be closed with the personnel center or passed back to the commander (or your replacement) for continued actions.

The Mission

The reader may think this section unnecessary, because it's assumed that everyone understands the unit's mission both in wartime and peacetime. Don't take this for granted. Understanding the mission of your squadron may not be as easy and clear as you might think, particularly in this twenty-first century environment of rapid change. Several commanders noted that not every member of the unit did, in fact, know what the squadron's true mission was and treated their service as just another "job." This breach needs to be identified early and corrected swiftly.

Colonel Klausner quickly found out that the vast majority of his squadron had little real idea of what the squadron's mission was. "I was flabbergasted. No one in the room during my first staff meeting had any idea of where we were going. I knew immediately that my short-term task was now defined."[7]

How did he attack this problem? He held a series of commander's calls where he clearly delineated the squadron's mission in terms that every airman and civilian could understand. He held them separately, in small groups divided by rank, so that he could ensure eye-to-eye contact with every member of the squadron. "Re-focusing the squadron on who we were and why we were there was relatively easy. They soon understood the mission and grasped their role in making it succeed. I watched the lightbulb click on."[8] It's imperative that every airman and officer who drives through the gate each morning understands that he or she is essential to the success of the squadron.

Without question, the bottom line for any military unit is its ability to perform its mission in peacetime or wartime. Your squadron's ability to accomplish any tasking can greatly depend on your personal expertise or knowledge of the mission. Although you may have been an operations officer or deputy commander whose primary duty was specifically to *oversee* the unit mission, as commander you are responsible *for* the mission. The difference can be daunting. Every single commander I interviewed agreed that the best method to lead the unit in its mission is simply to "lead the way and be out front" as much as possible. All of them ranked a complete understanding of the mission at the top of any list of a commander's priorities.

A commander also needs to understand that some circumstances will prevent him or her from performing certain tasks that the troops perform. For example, a rated officer who has taken over a maintenance squadron cannot reasonably be expected to possess the same knowledge and expertise as the senior maintenance supervisors. You will find it important to get out early during your command and learn the mission from your people, at all times of the day and night. Be humble. Ask questions. Let them teach *you*. A commander honest enough to admit he or she doesn't know it all wins a lot of respect from the troops.

A solid working knowledge of the mission means knowledge not only at your level as commander or your subordinates' level but also mission knowledge as it relates to your boss. The best way to gain this type of knowledge—how your boss views your mission—is by talking to him or her in some detail about the subject. It is imperative that you understand the commander's vision of where the group is headed and where he or she wants you to be focused in your squadron. It will parallel the mission of the wing and should be firmly entrenched in your mind as you steer your squadron forward in combat capability. One commander related how she scheduled herself on her boss's calendar the first day after taking command to learn exactly how he viewed the mission of her squadron. She ranked this as one of the smartest moves she made as commander.

Knowing the mission of the wing is also extremely important and where your squadron fits within it is critical for long-term goals. No squadron in the Air Force can successfully perform its mission alone; every unit requires help or support from other units and agencies on base. Gaining an early understanding of how the squadron fits into the overall wing mission will help the commander lead the unit. Many commanders noted that their indoctrination on this subject began during their first meeting with their wing commander and continued as they met the other group and squadron commanders on base.

The People

Although an entire chapter is devoted to the subject of people (chapter 3), this section specifically relates to the advice offered regarding the initial meetings you have with your squadron's personnel and the importance of making a first and lasting impression.

The only effective way you can really get to know the professionals who work for you is to get out of your office (something many commanders admitted was their overall greatest weakness), and do it often. The members of the squadron may not know who you are and may have only seen you once in their lives during your change of command ceremony.

You can also gain a quick snapshot of the squadron by obtaining a simple recall roster from your secretary or an Alpha roster from your orderly room. This will show you how the squadron is currently organized, who the key players are, and how the flights or divisions are formed. Conversely, as was the case with several commanders interviewed, you may need to reorganize or streamline your new squadron to fit a new aspect of your unit's mission.

The problem with many squadrons, particularly the ones that are failing, is that they tend to be overmanaged and underled. They may excel in the ability to handle the daily routine, yet never question whether the routine should be done at all. There is a profound difference between leadership and management, and both are important. *Good leadership* is what makes the difference between a squadron that just "gets by," and one that excels. Even the definitions speak volumes—to manage means to "bring about, to accomplish, to have charge of or responsibility for, to conduct." Leading is "influencing, guiding in direction,

---

Proverb for Leadership

People want direction. They want to be given challenging tasks, training in how to accomplish them, and the resources necessary to do them well. Effective leaders strive to create an environment of trust and understanding that encourages their subordinates to seize the initiative and act.[9]

---

course, action, opinion." The distinction is crucial. Leadership is what gives an organization its vision, its focus, and its ability to translate that vision into reality. As the squadron commander, you stand at the helm of the leadership agenda.

Former squadron commanders will tell you that knowing your people ranks on the same high level as knowing your unit's mission. Not only does the commander have to be knowledgeable of the strengths and weaknesses of unit personnel relative to mission accomplishment but also relative to their Air Force careers, and to some degree, their personal lives. Knowledge of each individual's personal and professional abilities will help the commander fully understand the squadron's overall capability. Knowledge of individual strengths and weaknesses relative to a successful career and individual desires is important because the commander is the unit's focal point. Finally, a general knowledge of his or her people's personal lives will allow the commander to identify and circumvent potential problems that can negatively influence mission accomplishment. None of this is an easy chore.

One former commander told me that before his PCS, he asked his new squadron to send a roster of all unit personnel and their families. Before he arrived at his new base, he attempted to learn as many names as he could so that when he first met the squadron members, he knew their first names, their spouse's names, and something about their families. It is not essential to go to such an effort, but, time permitting, it certainly sends a good message to a new squadron. As a minimum, it's recommended that you have a good grasp of your new squadron's senior leadership, both officer and enlisted.

Take the opportunity to sit down with your predecessor to discuss both mission and people. Such conferences are highly recommended, if possible. But one caution: while it's good to hear the outgoing commander's detailed assessment on the unit's personnel, you should not let it prejudice your opinion completely. Make a mental note of the comments, but wait and see how each individual performs under your command. Your personal leadership will make the difference.

One commander told me that he could get a feel for people's ability to perform the mission just by talking to them about it. He never specifically quizzed individuals on their duties but rather preferred to walk around his squadron and get into group discussions about the mission. This not only got him out of the office and around the unit, but it also enabled him to see how his personnel interacted with each other.

Nearly every flying squadron commander interviewed mentioned the fact that only now, some 10 years after the merging of aircraft maintenance with aircraft operations (in some major commands), do flying squadron commanders begin to understand the enlisted corps. Particularly in most flying squadrons today, the aviators are brought up in their stovepipe of flying operations and not given a great deal of experience, outside some flight commands, in working with enlisted personnel. Lt Col Lennie Coleman was fortunate to have two opportunities as a squadron commander. He commanded the 322d Training Squadron for USAF basic trainees at Lackland AFB, Texas, and then the 69th FS (F-16) at Moody AFB, Georgia. Colonel Coleman's experiences while commanding a basic training squadron proved invaluable. "I learned a great deal. I had just come off a tour with the USAF Thunderbirds when I got the call to command a training squadron. What a rush. With a great deal of senior noncommissioned officer (SNCO) leadership there, including a first sergeant and chief master sergeant, I was fortunate to 'go to school' with them. They taught me as much as they could about enlisted personnel, their particular relationships, heritage, and importance to the mission. There's no doubt that I was a much better commander later in my career because of those experiences."[10]

He also mentioned this could have been one of his greatest failures. He said, "Because I knew some aviators understood very little of the enlisted corps, I should have spent much more time mentoring them as I was mentored years earlier. It would be a shame if your first understanding of enlisted issues came five minutes after you took the guidon at your change of command."[11] It takes strength of character to admit that you don't know everything about everything, and to know when to ask for help and education. Pride can kill a commander as quickly, if not quicker, as ignorance.

> The greatest mistake a person can make in life is to be continually afraid you will make one.
>
> —Elbert Hubbard
> Magazine editor

Another terrific suggestion for flying squadron commanders came from one particular commander and was echoed by many more. Lt Col Robert Suminsby Jr. commanded the 492d FS (F-15E) at Royal Air Force (RAF) Lakenheath, United Kingdom. He said you need to "dress for success," an idea that strongly recommends the flying squadron commander wear the battle dress uniform (BDU) when not actively engaged in mission planning or flying. "This was the easiest method of establishing trust and building credibility with the enlisted personnel in my squadron,"[12] he said. Most of the aviator commanders interviewed said that they would usually find no more time than once or twice a week to fly given the demands of command. On their nonflying days, the commander wore the BDUs of the majority of the nonflying personnel in those squadrons that employed maintainers. "It sounds like a simple thing, but it hits a huge home run with the enlisted folks and the nonflying officers. Wearing a flight suit all the time distances the commander from many of the personnel in the squadron. When the enlisted personnel see their commander wearing a battle dress uniform, it sends the nonverbal message that the boss is on their team,"[13] said Colonel Suminsby.

I wholeheartedly agree. There were many days when I'd wear BDUs to present a Good Conduct medal for a young airman, switch to a service dress uniform to conduct an officer's promotion ceremony, and then change into a mess dress uniform for the evening's formal Airman Leadership School (ALS) graduation. Your squadron members see you daily and notice your concern for wearing the proper uniform for a given event. It's cheap, it's easy, and it causes no harm. Do it. "But do it right," said Lt Col Terry Kono, who commanded the 436th Training Squadron, Dyess AFB, Texas. "There is also a respect for the uniform that's often neglected in the rush to do the right thing. When a commander walks into the squadron with properly bloused pants, or properly rolled sleeves, or a nicely starched set, that also makes the impression that the commander respects the uniform, and expects everyone else to as well."[14]

The Change of Command Ceremony

It's finally here! The moment you've been waiting for has arrived, and it's time to enjoy the moment.

As the incoming commander, you will have your first opportunity to address the audience at the change of command ceremony. Apply the age-old "3:7 rule": the incoming commander should spend no more than three minutes on formal remarks after introductions, and the outgoing commander should spend no more than seven minutes on comments. In your remarks, be upbeat and positive. Be brief, thank the many people who have helped in the past, lay out a broad idea of where you want to lead the unit, recognize the accomplishments of the outgoing commander, and tell the unit how proud you are to join their squadron. After the change of command ceremony, it's time to enjoy the reception, party, or whatever—the hard work starts the next morning.

If you have the luxury of time to prepare your change of command remarks before you leave your last duty section, make sure you call up to your new wing's protocol office, or your new squadron secretary as appropriate, to get a list of the distinguished visitors who will be attending your ceremony. Ensure you follow normal protocol procedures by acknowledging the senior military and civilian guests who will be in attendance. This is not only an opportunity to recognize those important community leaders but gives you a short introduction to the key personnel you'll probably be meeting at your post-change of command reception.

Other than the above recommendations, I suggest you leave the details of the ceremony to your predecessor and the unit's desires. Nothing makes a negative impression quite like the incoming commander/spouse imposing excessive direction on the ceremony or reception. Humility is important, and doing the same at the end of your tour is also important. Be aware.

Another good idea is this: If time permits, have your current wing photo lab take a formal picture of you for posting at your new assignment. As will be discussed in chapter 7, "Finishing the Job and Leaving in Style," your predecessor may prompt you for several copies of your formal photograph so it can be posted around your new squadron building(s) immediately following the passing of the guidon. Having this photograph taken at your old base prior to your arrival mitigates the need to have it taken later. This sets the standard for your squadron personnel by having this task done right and on time. You don't want your squadron members to think of the new commander as an "empty picture frame."

The Chain of Command

Command relationships are important in every Air Force unit. Many commanders make a special effort to meet with their new bosses before the change of command. That way, the new commander knows from the start what is, and what is not, important to those up the chain of command. As one commander pointed out, scheduling this meeting early enabled him to begin his tenure fully aware of what had gone right and wrong before and in what direction he needed to point his new squadron.

Even if you're stationed at the same base as the new squadron commander, you will want to talk to your new chain of command about its views of your duties. This holds true even if you are not changing supervisors—your boss's view of you as a squadron commander will be significantly different from his or her expectations of you in your current assignment. Indeed, this can be vitally important to demonstrate that you understand the increased and changed responsibilities you are accepting.

The Base Environment

Colonel Coleman was in a fortunate situation. He had been stationed at Moody AFB, Georgia, and had held various leadership positions in the wing before he took command of his squadron. "Being there for a couple of years allowed me to fully understand the base environment before I took command. The wing's mission, its leadership, the group commander's relationships and the like were familiar to me, which helped a great deal when I needed their help downstream."[15] He found that having already established credibility with the wing leadership was to his advantage. Failure to establish this credibility could work to your detriment as well, depending on your personal situation.

Interestingly enough, one officer who was brought in from a different wing to take command of a squadron felt that his experience, coming in with no preconceived ideas and with a fresh slate, was actually a benefit. He spent a couple of weeks reading as much as he could and talking with as many people as possible to gain a better understanding of the base environment before he arrived. Although his information came through other people's filters, he found that arriving as an "objective outsider" was a positive aspect of getting started. This also happened to me, and I found it to be true. Wing commanders and group commanders sometime make an effort to hire from without—to get the fresh view and to avoid "inbreeding."

As best as you can, take every opportunity to visit other base agencies, many with which you probably don't have much experience. It's best to do this at your leisure—when it fits your schedule—than having to do it later when it most definitely does not, like in an emergency situation. Many wings will ensure that you have inbriefings from some of these agencies, but rarely is it enough for what you may need. Visit the Office of Special Investigations (OSI) detachment, go to the law enforcement entry desk at the Security Forces Squadron, visit the Airman's Attic to see what they offer for services—as a couple of suggestions. The more you familiarize yourself with who and where they are, and, most importantly, what services they provide, the better your ability will be as a squadron commander to provide assistance, comfort, and guidance to help someone in trouble or in need of help. Make a social visit to such base agencies as Military Equal Opportunity, Life Skills Support Center, Air Force Aid, and International Red Cross before you have to visit them professionally on behalf of one of your unit's members. A good and experienced secretary can help here as well (see "Your Secretary," chapter 3). Allow your secretary to help organize and guide you through the base agencies that may affect your squadron the most.

All commanders interviewed discussed the need to be sensitive to the situation of the departing commander. It's a bad idea to visit your new squadron before the change of command, and in rare instances, you should visit them only when invited by the outgoing commander. Some commanders were emphatic that you must never visit your new squadron before taking the guidon regardless of the incumbent's suggestion. Your presence can inhibit the departing commander's ability to lead, if you cast him or her as a lame duck. One officer said that every time he went into his new unit (before taking command), a small crowd would gather—people looking to get some early "face time" with the new boss. This is rarely a good idea.

One commander of a flying unit was the same unit's operations officer prior to taking command. This created a sensitive situation when he was put in charge of coordinating the outgoing commander's going-away party. Should he attend or not? Even though both of them and their spouses were good friends, he did not attend the function. "I felt that this was his party and my presence there would only draw attention away from his night. This was a party for him, and I didn't want my presence to detract from that." Sound advice.

One officer who was going "across the street" to take command of a sister squadron said that he was very careful what he said when asked what changes he had planned for his new unit. He felt the need to be totally positive towards his new unit and to avoid any comparisons to his old squadron. He also said that he felt the worst thing he could do before the change of command would be to talk about "turning his new

15

unit upside down." Therefore, even though he had some firm ideas on future changes, he kept them to himself until he was in charge—an attitude that can certainly do no harm and one that leaves the new commander in a position to act more confidently once he assumes command.

Lt Col David Hudson had a different problem adjusting to his base environment—or lack of one, as was his case. In command of the North Atlantic Treaty Organization (NATO) Airborne Warning and Control System (AWACS) Squadron 1 in Geilenkirchen, Germany, he had almost no base structure to rely upon. More than half his squadron was made up of NATO international personnel, and there was very little traditional base support. "This created all kinds of challenges," he remarked. "We had no base exchange or commissary, and only a very limited hospital clinic. If you wanted anything, you had to go to the Netherlands. It took me a while to get used to not having a normal Air Force base structure with which to work."[16] Like any good commander, he recognized the challenges, mitigated them to the best of his ability, and moved on to other matters.

The Art of Command

What about the art of command? How do you "study up" for your command duties? In our service, a squadron commander usually learns how to command by commanding. The Air Force hasn't had in the past nearly the emphasis on command training as does the Army, but it is gaining ground rapidly. Most Army, Navy, and Marine Corps squadron (equivalent) commanders are notified 18 months prior to taking command. During this time, they may attend three separate leadership and command courses to prepare for command duty. These courses stress the nature of command and, in most instances, include a full-blown command field exercise.

How do you make up the delta? By reading as much as you can about leadership and command, talking with your current and former commanders, and getting as much advice from others as possible. Spend some time reflecting on your past commanders and make notes regarding your impressions of their strengths and weaknesses. Mentally walk through any number of scenarios you might have to deal with in command, and make notes of pertinent actions you'll likely make to resolve these situations. I believe every officer should build a list, no more than one page or so, of personal leadership principles. Often referred to as "leadership vectors," they form a gospel for leadership—a simple framework from which to proceed.

Your Family

While we are talking about preparing for command, let's not forget your family. Their lives can change substantially as you take over your new responsibilities. Your spouse may also inherit some work and will not be paid one dime. One former Air Combat Command (ACC) squadron commander mentioned that she asked many questions upon arriving at her new base concerning any spouse responsibilities so that her spouse would not be blindsided when he arrived with the kids just before the big day. It's a real good idea to explain fully to your spouse what you've learned about your new squadron as you prepare for command. Don't forget your children, either. If they are old enough to understand, talk to them about your new duties and how your new position may affect them. Time will be precious.

Said Colonel Zastrow, "Prepare your family and home life for this new and challenging experience. Beyond preparing yourself, a commander must prepare his or her family for this unique, demanding timeframe. They need to have some idea of the level of responsibility that accompanies command. They deserve the forewarnings of the late night/early morning phone calls. The extensive preparation for no-notice generations or deployments, and the expectation of your long days plotting out and executing the success of your precious group of airmen."[17] Sound advice, for sure.

The First Three Months
(When the Honeymoon's Over!)

In late October 1947, Lt Col LeRoy Stefen wrote General of the Army Henry H. "Hap" Arnold regarding a question of leadership

17

(and implied command). General Arnold, having just retired from the Army Air Corps, spent two days a week in an office reserved for him at Hamilton Field, near San Francisco, handling a voluminous amount of correspondence. He believed the honors accorded him required this attention.

General Arnold's vision, articulated more than 50 years ago, continues to hold relevance in today's Air Force environment and continues to be a primer for those officers lucky enough to assume command. The original autographed letter is displayed under glass at the Air University Library, Air University, Maxwell AFB, Alabama.

His advice for command addressed to Colonel Stefen follows (verbatim):

<u>**COPY**</u>

HAMILTON FIELD, CALIFORNIA
Office of the General of the Army, H.H. Arnold
5 November 1947

In Reply Refer To:

Lt.Colonel LeRoy L. Stefen, A.C.,
641 Circle Drive
Palo Alto, Calif.

Dear Colonel Stefen:

Your recent question has so many ramifications, I can suggest but a few of what appear to be the most generally important requisites for a successful military career. Here they are:

1. **Basic knowledge. Exact, clear knowledge; not a hazy smattering. This kind of knowledge of the basics of your profession; of every assignment you are given, - this is your "technique"; this constitutes your "tools".**

2. **Hard work: unrelenting, hard work. Some persons have a natural capacity for it; others have to develop it. No outstanding success is ever achieved without it.**

3. **Vision.** The degree of vision depends, naturally, upon the quality of an individual's imagination; yet, one can train himself to look beyond his immediate assignment, to its relation to the next higher echelon of command, and the next, and the next, and, so on, to the highest level or overall sphere of activity of which he can envision its being a part. He can also, - if he has the capacity – envision possibilities yet undeveloped: new horizons of activity. This is the kind of vision that begets enthusiasm; and enthusiasm is the eager, driving force that converts dreams into realities.

4. **Judgement:** not only the judgement that makes quick, correct decisions, but the ability to judge human nature, as well. Putting the right men in the right places, - this is an essential in building a strong, successful; organization.

5. **Articulateness.** A comparatively overlooked factor, but, nevertheless, a most important one. Many an excellent idea is "stillborn" because its originator did not have the ability "to put it across". Public speaking courses are excellent aids in acquiring this faculty.

6. **Properly adjusted human relationships.** Naturally, this is largely a matter of personality: some persons just naturally get along with people; others, just as naturally, do not. But in the military sphere, if one is going "to get to first base", he must be able to handle men successfully. The study of psychology is undoubtedly a great practical help to those who find the matter of human relationships somewhat difficult; but I have also observed these things help: firmness, plus tolerance; sympathetic understanding of the little man's position and problems, as well as understanding of one's relation to the man at the top. Best of all, of course, is the practical application of the Golden Rule, - the simplest and the best code of ethics yet devised.

7. **Personal integrity. This covers a very wide field. To touch upon one or two, - it means, for example, maintaining the courage of one's convictions. By no means should this be confused with <u>stubborn</u> thinking. Stubborn thinking is as outmoded as the ox cart. Its exact opposite, resilient thinking, is Today's Must: a man must be able to accommodate his thinking quickly and accurately to <u>his</u> rapidly changing world; nevertheless, it must be his thinking, - not someone's else.**

> **Personal integrity also means moral integrity. Regardless of what appear to be some superficial ideas of present-day conduct, fundamentally, - today as always -, the man who is genuinely respected is the man who keeps his moral integrity sound; who is trustworthy in every respect. To be successful, a man must trust others; and a man cannot trust others, who does not trust himself.**

> **These are but a few thoughts. When it comes right down to "brass tacks", however, in the military field, as in all other fields, it would seem to be a man's native ability that spells the difference between failure and mediocrity; between mediocrity and success. Two men may work equally hard toward a common goal; one will have just that "something" the other lacks, that puts him on the top. This is the intangible, - the spirit of a man.**

> **With very best wishes for your success,**
>
> **Sincerely yours,**
>
> **/signed/**
>
> **H. H. Arnold,**
>
> **General of the Army.**

(Note: This letter typed from signed original; no punctuation or grammar changed.)[18]

Your Position as Commander

When things go wrong in your command, start searching for the reason in increasingly larger concentric circles around your own desk.

—Gen Bruce C. Clark
Commander in Chief of the US
Army in Europe, 1960–62

"Your whole world expands when you become a commander," remarked Colonel Isola. "I remember sitting in many squadron audiences as a young officer, looking up to the commander. I truly didn't understand how much responsibility fell on him. I had to learn pretty quickly. It's important to step back and look at the whole forest and not at a couple of trees."[19]

Never forget that you now live in a fish bowl—all eyes are on you. People will look at you in a light you're not used to nor probably comfortable with. It all comes with the territory. The troops are watching your every move, inside and outside the squadron. Every member of your unit will look up to you for guidance and leadership, and it will be your daily actions that will speak the loudest. What you do will be more important than what you say. The old adage of "do as I say, not as I do" will have no place in the command of an Air Force squadron because your squadron members are adults, not children. They are very smart and will see through any veil of insincerity quickly, which will lead to your loss of credibility and respect.

Lt Col Rollins Hickman had the great fortune of commanding a large Security Forces squadron not once, but three times. After successful tours in command of the 355th Security Forces Squadron (SFS), Davis–Monthan AFB, Arizona; the 90th SFS, F. E. Warren AFB, Wyoming; and the 4406th(P) SFS, Kuwait; he had a lot of advice to offer a new commander. One thing he emphasized repeatedly was the fact that you truly live in a "glass house" as a commander, "inside and outside the squadron, on- and off- duty, 24/7," said Colonel Hickman. He offered this advice regarding informal discussions and implicit policy decisions, "Be very careful of what you say and do, particularly outside the confines of your office. Many troops will try to

Proverb for Command

It's your job to ensure the mission gets done, and you certainly can't do it without the personnel in your command. Loyalty works both ways — up and down the chain of command. Just as you owe your unfettered opinion to your boss, and have the moral courage to disagree with him privately, you must also express the same courage to your personnel. Your squadron doesn't operate in a vacuum and neither should you. Encourage debate and differing opinions from those who offer counsel and advice. Think carefully about every side of the issue, and then make a decision. Loyalty to superiors and subordinates does much more than ensure smooth-running peacetime organizations. It prepares units for combat operations by building trust in leaders and leader's faith in your airmen.[20]

get you to make policy statements while you're simply walking down the hallway or working out in the gym. Whether intentional or not, the word gets around quickly that you 'approved' something without it having been formally staffed. A simple comment from you, as the commander, can make a big difference now, and cause a lot of headaches later."[21]

Another piece of advice for your early weeks in command is to spend some time walking through your buildings and workspaces during the solitude of a weekend. Do so with a jaundiced eye toward detail. Study the bulletin boards. Are there outdated policy letters hanging on the corkboard? Do they have the signature of your predecessor? Is the standard wing inspector general (IG) letter up to date with the current IG? Is last month's holiday party advertisement still tacked to the wall? Replace them—all of them—with your policy letters, up-coming events, and so forth.

Take a look at your facility. Is it in need of repair? Do the doors need to be painted, the walls repaired, the restrooms refinished, the carpets cleaned or replaced? Does the exterior need policing of trash, blown debris, or old equipment? Now is the time to make those changes. Before too long, you will have been part of the squadron lifestyle to the degree that you'll overlook such eye-sores because you're accustomed to them. Make inquiries of your fellow civil engineering squadron commander for major re-pairs. Look at your squadron budget for allowances to complete self-help projects where available. If necessary, have a "stand down" day for a squadron-wide clean up of the entire area. There may be some quiet grumbling (sometimes maybe not so quiet) but in the long run, everyone likes, and deserves, a clean, com-fortable, and safe environment to work in.

Maj Jay Carroll commanded the 28th Security Forces Squadron at Ellsworth AFB, South Dakota. As the commander, he took a hard look at his facilities when he arrived on base. One thing he noticed missing in his squadron was a "com-mander's corner," a bulletin board located where everyone in the squadron would see it as they came to and from work. "I thought it important to have a bulletin board behind encased glass where I would post the most important, current infor-mation for those who had a minute to read. I put letters of commendation and appreciation, promotion lists, recognition items, and pictures of special events. Before too long, it be-came a gathering place."[22]

Without question, be honest and up front with your squadron at every instance. It may be difficult at times, but it will be the right thing to do in the end. Sugarcoating bad news never works. Colonel Coleman once volunteered his fighter squadron to deploy to Operation Southern Watch to relieve his sister squadron that had been there indefinitely. "Although I knew the deployment was the right thing to do, I also knew it wouldn't go over very well with the majority of my squadron. We hadn't deployed in some time and had nothing on the hori-zon. I felt we needed to exercise our deployment capability, and I knew we could have used the training. It was a tough

---

Proverb for Command

People of integrity consistently act according to principles—not just what might work at the moment. Leaders of integrity make their principles known and consistently act in accordance with them. You're honest to others by not presenting yourself or your actions as anything other than what they truly are. Say what you mean and mean what you say. If you can't accomplish a mission, inform your chain of command. If you inadvertently pass on bad information, correct it as soon as you find out it's wrong. People of integrity do the right thing not because it's convenient or because they have no choice. They choose the right thing because their character permits no less. Conducting yourself with integrity has three parts: Separating what's right from what's wrong, acting according to what you know to be right, even at personal cost, and saying openly that you're acting on your understanding of right versus wrong.[23]

---

decision, but I knew I had to tell my squadron up front that it was I who volunteered our deployment, and not blame it on 'the schedule.'"[24]

Your Office Hours

By far, one of the most contentious subjects amongst the scores of former squadron commanders interviewed dealt with the public perception issue of office hours. Is it better to work from 0800 to 1700 every day or from 0430 to 2100 every day? While there was no consensus on this issue, one thing stood out very clearly—your hours will be long, both through the

24

week and through the weekend, in many instances. The question is how do you deal with it? What perception do you strive to give your squadron?

Lt Col Alan Hunt commanded the 13th Airlift Squadron (C-141) at McGuire AFB, New Jersey. He took the view that he didn't want to be seen at the office much after normal working hours because he knew that his senior officers and NCOs would be watching. The signal he wanted to send was "go home to your families." "Not only are first impressions important, all impressions are important. If they were to see my car in the parking lot when they came to work, and see it again when they left for the evening, it sends the impression that work is more important than family or other social endeavors. Even though they probably knew I was taking work home at night, I felt it was the better thing to do."[25]

Another commander shared a different view. Much of her job as the commander of an intelligence squadron included classified material, which she couldn't take home. She therefore spent the bulk of her day behind the desk and computer. She, too, had a family waiting at home every night but didn't want to take other work home because that would send the wrong signal to her family—that her work was more important than the few hours she had with her family every day. "My family would rather I stay at the squadron to get the necessary day's work complete before coming home. That way, they knew that when I walked in the door it was their time, and not extended work time," she said.

Either way, the choice will be yours and will, as many other things, be dictated by the scope of your particular responsibilities of command. But if you do have a choice, make a conscious effort to explain to both your squadron and your family the reasons behind your modus operandi. If you choose to put in long hours at your squadron, it might be a good idea to mention the fact (at a commander's call, for example) that your choice should not be taken as a lead for the squadron. Assure your squadron personnel that you do not expect anyone to stay at their desks late so as not to be seen leaving before the commander. Create a climate of honesty and understanding within your unit, and the rewards will be great down the road.

You as the Leader

One of the attributes of effective leadership at the squadron commander level is the ability and vision to keep the forest in sight when everyone else is looking at the trees. The talent to gain and keep such a perspective is an essential ingredient of leadership.

Proverb for Leadership

Leadership is influencing people—by providing purpose, direction, and motivation—while operating to accomplish the mission and improving the organization.[26]

More than a decade ago a book about "command" was written by Col John G. Meyer Jr., USA, entitled *Company Command—The Bottom Line.* It is essentially a similar book of advice written from one officer's perspective about how to command at the Army company level. With his principal audience being a junior to mid-grade captain, he offers this perspective of a former Army battalion commander who commanded a group of infantrymen. While it may not have any direct relevance to you and your squadron, at least his words do make you think. I've paraphased them to read in Air Force parlance. He writes,

> The commander's juxtaposition was inherent in "old think" perspective. He said, Whom do we admire? We admire the man with "guts." What do we really mean by this? We mean the man who drives his people hard, who has the reputation for firing subordinates, who goes for the jugular, who works his people 14 hours a day, and who takes his objective in spite of heavy and possibly unnecessary casualties. We set these people up and idolize them. Even in industry. We like the kind of guy who moves in as the CEO and fires three-fourths of the vice presidents in the first week. He gets things done! He's got guts![27]

But what about the perceptive, cool-headed leader who takes a group or individuals and molds them into an effective, highly spirited team of war fighters? Or, the colonel who can see the great potential of a young commander who is performing only marginally, and, through encouraging and mentoring, turns him into a first-rate performer? Or, the leader in combat who takes his objective with no casualties? Or, the squadron commander who has the guts to resist the arbitrary, capricious order of a group commander to fire a faltering flight commander because the colonel believes that with proper leadership that flight commander can be made into a successful one? Or, the Air Staff division chief who defies the norm and refuses to arrive at his office before 0730 or to require his action officers to do so and who manages the workload of his division so that every man gets a reasonable amount of leave, seldom has to work on weekends, and gets home every evening at a reasonable hour?

We seldom hear about those people. We don't hold them up as examples as we should. The higher we go, the more important it is to be careful that our impact on the lives and careers and families of our subordinates is positive and not negative. I can think of a division artillery commander in Germany who ruled by fear, who was hated by his subordinates, and who was the proximate cause of a number of serious domestic crises. I can think of a lieutenant general in the Pentagon who purposely intimidated his subordinates and associates to get his own way. I can think of a colonel, the executive to a former chief of staff, who blossomed like a rose to his superiors, but who was vicious, demeaning, and bullying to his subordinates. I can think of a colonel in the Pentagon who never showed appreciation and voiced only criticism and whose subordinates gradually became discouraged and frustrated and unproductive.

In stark contrast, I remember a lieutenant general whose modus operandi was to make his subordinates successful in their jobs. He said,

> I'll have no problem with my job if I can make all of my subordinates successful. I remember a squadron commander in Germany with whom I was closely associated who spent countless hours talking with subordinates at every level, coaching them, encouraging them, and teaching them. I think of an Air Staff division chief who looked for opportunities to push his action officers into the limelight, who volunteered them for prestigious positions as secretarial-level 'horse holders,' who worked in the background to cross-train his people so that no one

27

would ever have to be called back from leave, who personally took the rap when things went wrong, and who, in my opinion, ran the best division in the Pentagon. It all gets back to how they looked at people, their value, their dignity, their fundamental worth, their potential.[28]

Effective squadron commanders act competently and confidently. Your very attitude will set the tone for the entire squadron, and it is you alone who chooses your attitude—day to day, task to task, even minute to minute. Remember that optimism, a positive outlook, and a sense of humor is infectious. If given the chance to view a situation as with the glass half-empty or half-full—choose half-full.

You'll begin to understand something about how your new position affects the others the first morning you walk into the squadron after your change of command. Regardless of how you find out, one thing you will quickly understand about your new position is that you are no longer "one of the gang." Distancing yourself as the commander on a professional basis is important, not only for you but also for your subordinates. It's imperative that you avoid any perception of favoritism towards any of your unit's personnel. This will only lead to poor order and morale on the part of many. Find the balance and stick to it.

Another fact that a commander has to accept quickly—command is a 24-hour-a-day, seven-day-a-week job that allows for less personal freedom than most other duties. I found this true—in many ways you'll feel married to the squadron.

Besides understanding how your new command position affects unit personnel, you'll likely also notice changes in your peer group and your relationship with your boss. You will quickly find your peer group to be the other squadron commanders on base. Because of the uniqueness of squadron command, the only other officers who could fully understand and appreciate your responsibilities and span of authority are other commanders. Work hard to get together with this group of fellow commanders, both professionally and socially. Include the spouses as well. The relationships you foster with this group will help you during your tour of command; these will be officers whose paths you may cross again in your Air Force career. You are the vital link between all other wing organizations and every single individual in your unit.

Proverb for Command

Your span of influence, those lives you can reach out
and touch, can range from a few dozen to a few hundred people. Until now, you have likely been the dutiful follower in one sense and a direct leader in another.
Regardless, now as the commander, your leadership
style must shift in its focus to an organizational one in
which your leadership style will be indirect. You must
establish policies and foster the organizational climate
that supports the squadron's mission. Organizational
leadership skills differ from direct leadership skills in
degree, but not in kind. That is, the skill domains are
the same, but organizational leaders must deal with
more complexity, more people, greater uncertainty,
and a greater number of unintended consequences.[29]

Once you understand your role and the idea that you now
work in a "glass house," how do you act in this environment?
The best solution here is perhaps the simplest one: You don't
change! One of the best pieces of advice I ever received came
from my wing commander. He told me not to change a thing
when I took command. He said that what I had done to get me
to this position would keep me in good stead during my command. He also told me not to attempt to command like my
predecessor, but to run the squadron as I saw fit. Don't try to
be someone else. Be yourself.

*Victory smiles upon those who anticipate the changes in the
character of war, not upon those who wait to adapt themselves after the changes occur.*
                                            —Giulio Douhet

29

Articulate Your Vision

Ensuring every member of your squadron understands your vision of where you want the squadron to go may be a challenge. Simply telling your senior staff the goals for the future may not be good enough. A great piece of "vision" advice came from Lt Col Alan Gross, who commanded the 10th Intelligence Squadron, Langley AFB, Virginia. "Publish your vision. You go to all the trouble of defining your vision of where you want the squadron to go, and you probably mentioned it in your change of command speech or at your first commander's call, but that's not enough. Too many people tend to forget what was said yesterday, and your vision as the commander is too important not to have everyone's attention. Publish your leadership philosophy for all to see. Bulletin boards throughout the squadron provide a good place for those to read."[30]

Colonel Gross' published philosophy is listed below.

1. **People First.** People are our number one asset and deserve the best we can give them. Motivated personnel have made the difference and have overcome great odds throughout history. You are this organization, and I promise to dedicate myself in allowing you to "be all you can be."

2. **Integrity.** This is a core value that must guide our interaction to build mutual trust and respect. We must be able to count on each other to say what we mean and do what we say. We must then be accountable for our actions and decisions.

3. **Competence.** This is the bond that ties us together and to the American people. Each of you is already a master of your job, and I'm counting on your expertise! I also expect you to grow within our profession of arms—the American people deserve nothing less!

4. **Courage.** Physical and moral courage are essential to success in military operations. We must be willing to make sacrifices for each other and the nation. We must also be willing to stand up for what we believe is right, even if that stand is unpopular. Each of you have an obligation to provide me your full and candid opinions when alternative actions are being considered and to provide your complete loyalty once decisions are made.

5. **Teamwork.** This is the centerpiece of our operations. Our ultimate success or failure truly relies on this concept, and I expect all of you to lead by example. We are also part of a larger team that demands war-fighting participation and not just support. Teamwork in our profession of arms is not just a cliché, it is our key to success!

6. **Initiative.** Simply put, initiative wins wars and creates nations! You need to take advantage of every situation to improve upon it, and strive to be better every day. Work hard to improve yourself, the squadron, and to become "all you can be." Bottom line: it is incumbent on everyone to be part of the solution, not part of the problem![31]

I promise you my complete devotion and to always do my best . . . and I expect the same from you!

Lt Col Alan Gross
Commander
10th Intelligence Squadron

Unit "Health"

A great way to get an independent, objective look at the health of your squadron is to ask the Military Equal Opportunity (MEO) office to conduct a Unit Climate Assessment (UCA). As of this writing, all wing MEO offices are required to conduct a UCA within the first six months of your command. They are particularly adept at determining the health of your unit. Depending on the size of your squadron, they may take only one day or several days to assess your squadron. They use a battery of questionnaires, conduct interviews, and freely walk throughout your squadron talking with the personnel whom you command.

One word of note: Ensure you understand that a UCA is only a snapshot of your squadron at any given time. Don't give it tremendous weight, but do take into account there will always be some squadron members who take up space at both ends of the assessment—overly positive and overly negative. Discard both when considering major changes. The professionals who administered the assessment will definitely follow up with an outbrief to you, and only you. The results will not be published for the squadron's review, nor will it be forwarded to your boss. The purpose of this assessment is for you to gauge where your squadron is and give you a reference point—based on the findings—of where you need to go. It is not a referendum on your leadership; it's a tool you use to pinpoint any problem areas.

Colonel Hickman was a fan of UCAs and offered this advice: "The UCA belongs to the squadron, and as such, is there for your careful review. If a UCA was recently accomplished, by all means read it carefully. If a copy isn't in a drawer in your new desk, the wing MEO will have a filed copy for your review. Take the candid comments with a grain of salt—and don't spend too much time or effort with the obvious disgruntled comments, if any, but capture the overall health of the unit. This will give you a look at where the members of your squadron think they are in life and gives you a starting point from which to chart a new course."[32] For example, if there are a number of comments remarking that the former squadron leadership failed to recognize good work and had a poor squadron awards and decorations program, you might take this information as a point to bring up with your staff in the first few staff meetings. Ask the hard questions: Is this a valid critique? What formal recognition programs do we have in place? If we aren't doing enough, what more can we do? Your staff will soon see that your interest is in the morale and welfare of the squadron personnel, and it will likely manifest itself in your senior staff's interest as well.

Of the scores of commanders who responded to this subject, the answers were greatly varied as to when you should ask for a UCA after assuming command. As mentioned above, the UCA by regulation is supposed to be taken within the first six months of command, but this can be waived to a later time by you, given appropriate circumstances. Some thought a good rule of thumb was to have one conducted shortly after you've come on board (inside of three months) to give you a snapshot of where the squadron currently is (and presumably was under the command of your predecessor) and to allow you the most time to make course corrections. Others thought quite differently. Many of these people thought that you should ask for a UCA no sooner than six months, and more agreed to a nine-month time frame to allow you, as commander, to make changes as you've seen fit. "I asked for a UCA at the nine-month point for a good reason. I set the direction of my squadron very early, and figured that a good six months or more was needed for it to set in with the unit personnel. By the nine-month period I was sure that any comments received were for me and not my predecessor,"[33] said Colonel Isola. Some believed that taking the survey results at the one-third mark in your tenure better assesses the squadron and how it has been operating under your command. This, they felt, gave a more accurate assessment of not only the squadron as a whole, but your performance as commander.

Colonel Hunt had a different perspective and offered this advice, "As the outgoing commander, have a UCA performed for the benefit of the incoming commander. Every commander can't be everything to every one. You can't do it all (well). It'll help him set his priorities."[34]

Many times a new commander will inherit a squadron that performs its mission well and has high morale. In this fortunate case, few if any course corrections are required immediately after taking the reins of command. As the old saying goes, "if it ain't broke, don't fix it." But don't take your eye off it, either.

> Difficulties always arise from attempts to improve to the point of achieving what is not possible, thereby failing to gain what is well within reach.

> —J. M. Cameron
> Photographer

Shortly after taking over such a unit, one lieutenant colonel told her entire squadron that she knew they performed well and that she would adapt to the unit first before making any adjustments to fit her style as time went on. This was very well received, and she quickly gained the confidence of her supervisors. Most former commanders agreed that changing things right away just for the sake of change was not a good idea.

Other new commanders inherit squadrons in trouble. This is a particularly good time for you to spend some time with your group commander. It is times like these when you may very well have to come into the squadron with a clear and un-ambiguous style that ensures everyone knows that a significant change is in order. This, unlike the former example, will require a greater deal of consideration before you make your first move. Don't be afraid that you'll be viewed as a "tough guy." If your squadron is in trouble, every member will know it, and will even more so be looking to you and your leadership to guide them through the necessary changes. Every member of your unit wants to be part of the best squadron on base, and it's your job to lead them to heights yet unseen. Again, your group commander can be an excellent source of advice. The severity of the problems will force you to act quickly, but this method of approaching the situation will win you the confidence and respect of your people.

Some squadrons may not be in severe trouble but may be "down" for one reason or another. One squadron, for example, was in great shape except for its facility. The squadron was functioning well and unit morale was high, but many members felt the building was a disgrace. The new commander put this on the top of his priority list, worked closely with the civil engineering squadron commander, and finally initiated a self-help program that turned his building into one of the best on base. This improved unit morale and positively influenced mission performance.

"Facility planning and future improvements are key duties of the squadron commander. Rarely is any other particular person tasked to work long-term strategic issues of facility requirements. When you take command, you not only get the mission and the personnel—you may get multiple facilities as well, and the squadron commander is the one who needs to look out for the long-term interests for his squadron,"[35] added Lt Col Jay Carlson, who commanded the 18th Contracting Squadron, Kadena AB, Japan.

> *The very essence of leadership is that you have to have a vision.*
>
> —Theodore Hesburgh
> President Emeritus
> University of Notre Dame

Setting the Direction

Col Mark Browne had a tremendous challenge ahead of him in his command of a recruiting squadron. But that didn't stop him from charting the course of his unit. "It all began with integrity, something that in the recruiting business, to be quite frank, is an everyday test. The pressure on our young recruiters is intense. Not because our recruiters have less integrity, but their jobs are in an unbelievably stressful environment with never-ending goals and requirements. I was constantly treading the battle line between the mental and emotional perspectives."[36] But he established the direction and kept the vision of the squadron in front of his personnel constantly, "sometimes to the point where they were getting sick of it. But every airman knew the mission of the squadron and what his place was in ensuring we met our goals. And we did."[37]

Another commander of a training squadron related that he would first get his squadron's members to "buy into" his overall game plan before formally instituting changes. Early in his command, he recognized a span of control problem and felt it was wise to increase the number of separate squadron flights. Instead of dictating this change, he asked the squadron members for some advice concerning the possible organizational change. He already knew the answer would come back positive because it meant adding more flight commanders and other supervisory positions, but he wanted the squadron to feel a part of the decision. He also wanted to know if there were any potential problems with these moves that he might have overlooked. The unit personnel were very much in favor of the moves, and after receiving the positive feedback, the commander instituted the changes that improved mission effectiveness and unit morale.

Many commanders set the direction for their squadron by what is often called "focusing" the unit on certain priorities. The word should be used to focus your squadron on ensuring that they concentrate their efforts on the unit mission. The primary focus should be far above all other efforts of the squadron, and training should occupy as much of the commander's, deputy commander's, and flight commander's or flight chief's time. You, the commander, must insist that the actual squadron mission training remain on the top of your large pile of taskings.

One commander focused a portion of his attention on the conduct of his unit's internal business. One of his first changes was to give his supervisors a chance to supervise and not be micromanaged by the commander. He emphasized to his entire unit the concept of solving problems inside the squadron as opposed to taking them up the chain to his boss. When faced with difficulties, he urged everyone to "be part of the solution, not part of the problem." These directions were all designed to improve the unit's internal operations.

Sometimes the commander sees the need to direct his squadron outward. One such commander thought she needed to raise her squadron's self-confidence. To achieve this, she developed a large public relations effort to get the many accomplishments of her unit and its members recognized by the wing and local community. She used the base and community newspapers not only to publicize the achievements of unit members but also to educate the public on the squadron's operations. Once this program was fully implemented, she saw a marked improvement in the squadron's confidence and performance.

The toughest road to travel is setting the direction of a unit that is really in trouble. Often a new commander discovers many reasons the squadron is failing. A few guidelines for this type of situation follow:

1. Seek out and emphasize the good points to give people a hope for the future.

2. Believe your instincts and don't be afraid to make significant changes.

3. Listen to your boss's guidance.

4. Do not hesitate to fire people when necessary, but do so only as a last resort (and make it clear to them why they are being removed).

Within the first three months of their command tours, all of the commanders interviewed clearly understood they were the focal point for the unit; therefore, all squadron personnel looked to them for unambiguous direction. Your squadron needs a leader out front, not a manager behind the desk.

Colonel Zastrow offers the reader the personal checklist he referred to during his tenure in command.

Preparation—Personal Readiness for Command

1. Develop a commander's mind-set.
2. Build a command framework—organize your observations, beliefs, and thoughts.
3. Get physically, mentally, emotionally, and spiritually ready.
4. Prepare your family and home life.

Transition—Accepting the Guidon of Command

1. Strive for a smooth transition.
2. Planning/surviving the change of command.

Execution—Setting the Tone

1. Listen, understand, plan, then change.
2. Become a tactical strategist—learn unit mission, strategy/practices, and assets.
3. Adopt a confident, positive daily attitude.
4. Instill core values.
5. Lead by example.
6. Trust your guts and your people.
7. Ensure mission accomplishment.
8. Take care of your people.
9. Learn to lead (but don't do) in handling the details of your mission/trade/business.
10. Communicate, communicate, communicate.
11. Lead productive meetings—get rid of or change unproductive ones.
12. Demonstrate loyalty—in 3D.
13. Integrate with your peers.
14. Conquer adversity.

Sustainment—Running a Marathon, Not a Sprint

1. Maintain stamina and focus.
2. Learn to manage organizational stress.
3. Keep the mission fresh while praising accomplishments.
4. Innovate, integrate, and deliver impact.

Termination/Transition—Change of the Guard

1. Prepare your squadron—bridge the change of commanders.

2. Prepare your successor.

3. Exit quietly.

Notes

1. Army Field Manual (FM) 22-100, *Army Leadership,* 31 August 1999.

2. Lt Col Roderick Zastrow, interviewed by author, Maxwell Air Force Base (AFB), Ala., 3 May 2002.

3. Ibid.

4. Lt Col Kurt Klausner, interviewed by author, Maxwell AFB, Ala., 31 August 2001.

5. Ibid.

6. Col Mark Browne, interviewed by author, Maxwell AFB, Ala., 4 September 2001.

7. Klausner interview.

8. Ibid.

9. FM 22-100.

10. Lt Col Leonard Coleman, interviewed by author, Maxwell AFB, Ala., 30 August 2001.

11. Ibid.

12. Lt Col Robert Suminsby Jr., interviewed by author, Maxwell AFB, Ala., 25 January 2002.

13. Ibid.

14. Lt Col Terry Kono, interviewed by author, Dyess AFB, Tex., 20 December 2001.

15. Coleman interview.

16. Lt Col David Hudson, interviewed by author, Maxwell AFB, Ala., 3 December 2001.

17. Lt Col Roderick Zastrow, interviewed by author, Maxwell AFB, Ala., 14 May 2002.

18. Gen H. "Hap" Arnold, retired, to Lt Col Leroy Stefen, A.C., letter, subject: Leadership, 5 November 1947 (Maxwell AFB, Ala.: Air University Library), 4 October 2001.

19. Lt Col Eileen Isola, interviewed by author, Maxwell AFB, Ala., 5 September 2001.

20. FM 22-100.

21. Lt Col Rollins Hickman, interviewed by author, Maxwell AFB, Ala., 16 November 2001.

22. Maj Jay Carroll, interviewed by author, Maxwell AFB, Ala., 14 February 2002.

23. FM 22-100.

24. Coleman interview.

25. Lt Col Alan Hunt, interviewed by author, Maxwell AFB, Ala., 20 September 2001.

26. FM 22-100.

27. John G. Meyer Jr., and Gen Creighton Abrams, USA, *Company Command—The Bottom Line* (Washington, D.C.: National Defense University Press, Fort Lesley J. McNair, 1990).

28. Ibid.

29. FM 22-100.

30. Lt Col Alan Gross, interviewed by author, Maxwell AFB, Ala., 27 February 2002.

31. Ibid.

32. Hickman interview.

33. Isola interview.

34. Hunt interview.

35. Lt Col Jay Carlson, interviewed by author, Maxwell AFB, Ala., 20 September 2001.

36. Browne interview.

37. Ibid.

Chapter 2

The Mission

Of the many great military leaders in American history, Joshua L. Chamberlain was arguably one of the greatest. His actions, captured in print and in the motion picture film *Gettysburg*, should be studied. The following vignette references the early July 1863 Civil War battle at Gettysburg, Pennsylvania. Highlighted are some of the tenets of command that still apply today.

Lessons of Leadership in Action

In late June 1863, Gen Robert E. Lee's Army of Northern Virginia passed through Maryland and invaded Pennsylvania. For five days, the Army of the Potomac hurried to get between the Confederates and the national capital. On 1 July, the 20th Maine received word to press on to Gettysburg. The Union Army had engaged the Confederates there, and Union commanders were hurrying all available forces to the hills south of the little town.

The 20th Maine arrived at Gettysburg near midday on 2 July, after marching more than 100 miles in five days. They had only two hours sleep and no hot food during the past 24 hours. The regiment was preparing to go into a defensive position as part of the brigade when a staff officer rode up and began gesturing towards a little hill at the extreme southern end of the Union line. The hill, Little Round Top, dominated the Union position and, at that moment, was unoccupied. If the Confederates placed artillery on it, they could force the entire Union Army to withdraw. The hill had been left unprotected by a series of mistakes—wrong assumptions, the failure to communicate clearly, and the failure to check—and the situation was critical.

Realizing the danger, Colonel Vincent ordered his brigade to occupy Little Round Top. He positioned the 20th Maine, commanded by Lt Col Joshua L. Chamberlain, on his brigade's left flank, the extreme left of the Union line. Col Vincent ordered Lt Col Chamberlain to "hold at all hazards."

On Little Round Top, **Lieutenant Colonel Chamberlain told his company commanders the purpose and importance of their mission.** *He ordered the right flank company to tie in with the 83d Pennsylvania and the left flank company to anchor on a large boulder. His thoughts turned to the left flank. There was nothing there except a small hollow and the rising slope of Big Round Top. The 20th Maine was literally at the end of the line.*

Lt Col Chamberlain then showed a skill common to good tactical leaders. He imagined threats to his unit, did what he could do to guard against them, and considered what he would do to meet other possible threats. *Since his left flank was open, Lieutenant Colonel Chamberlain sent B Company, commanded by Capt Walter G. Morrill, off to guard it and "act as the necessities of the battle required." The captain positioned his men behind a stone wall that would face the flank of any Confederate advance. There, 14 soldiers from the 2d US sharpshooters, who had been separated from their unit, joined them.*

The 20th Maine had been in position only a few minutes when the soldiers of the 15th and 47th Alabama attacked. The Confederates also had marched all night and were tired and thirsty. Even so, they attacked ferociously.

The Maine men held their ground, but then one of Lt Col Chamberlain's officers reported seeing a large body of Confederate soldiers moving laterally behind the attacking force. **Lt Col Chamberlain climbed on a rock – exposing himself to enemy fire –** *and saw a Confederate unit moving around his exposed left flank. If they outflanked him, his unit would be pushed off its position and destroyed. He would have failed his mission.*

Lt Col Chamberlain had to think fast. The tactical manuals he so diligently studied called for a maneuver that would not work on this terrain. He had to create a new maneuver, one that his soldiers could clearly understand and execute, and execute now.

The 20th Maine was in a defensive line, two ranks deep. It was threatened by an attack around its left flank. So the colonel ordered his company commanders to stretch the line to the left and bend it back to form an angle, concealing the maneuver by keeping up a steady rate of fire. Now [Lt] Col Chamberlain's thin line was only one rank deep. His units, covering twice their normal frontage, were bent back into an L shape. Minutes after repositioning his force, the Confederate infantry, moving up to what they thought was an open flank, were thrown back by the redeployed left wing of the 20th Maine. Surprised and angry, they nonetheless attacked again.

The Maine men rallied and held their ground; the Confederates regrouped and attacked. "The Alabamians drove the Maine men from their positions five times. Five times they fought their way back again. At some places, the muzzles of the opposing guns almost touched." Lieutenant Colonel Chamberlain saw that he could not stay where he was and could not withdraw. So he decided to counterattack. His men would have the advantage of attacking down the steep hill, he reasoned, and the Confederates would not be expecting it. **Clearly he was risking his entire unit, but the fate of the Union Army depended on his men.**

The decision left Lieutenant Colonel Chamberlain with another problem: there was nothing in his tactics book about how to get his unit from its L-shaped position into a line of advance. Under tremendous fire and in the midst of battle, **Lt Col Chamberlain again called his commanders together. He explained that the regiment's left wing would swing around "like a barn door on a hinge" until it was even with the right wing.** Then the entire regiment, bayonets fixed, would charge downhill, staying anchored to the 83d Pennsylvania on its right. **The explanation was clear and the situation clearly desperate.**

When Lt Col Chamberlain gave the order, Lt Holman Melcher of F Company leaped forward and led the left wing downhill toward the surprised Confederates. Lt Col Chamberlain had positioned himself at the center of the L. When the left wing was abreast of the right wing, he jumped off the rock and led the right wing down the hill. **The entire regiment was now**

charging on line, swinging like a great barn door – just as its commander intended.

The Alabama soldiers, stunned at the sight of the charging Union troops, fell back on the positions behind them. There the 20th Maine's charge might have failed if not for a surprise resulting from Lieutenant Colonel Chamberlain's foresight. Just then Capt Morrill's B Company and the sharpshooters opened fire on the Confederate flank and rear. The exhausted and shattered Alabama regiments thought they were surrounded. They broke and ran, not realizing that one more attack would have carried the hill.

The slopes of Little Round Top were littered with bodies. Saplings halfway up the hill had been sawed in half by weapons fire. A third of the 20th Maine had fallen. Nonetheless, the farmers, woodsman, and fishermen from Maine **– under the command of a brave and creative leader who had anticipated enemy actions, improvised under fire, and applied disciplined initiative in the heat of the battle – had fought through to victory.** (Emphasis added.)[1]

This short story of Colonel Chamberlain's exploits sums up what many new commanders will face when in command—the uncertain and the unknown.

Command Relationships

The squadron's primary mission needs to be a commander's number one priority, since many factors affect a unit's ability to perform its mission effectively. Regarding unit effectiveness, the relationships your squadron—and you—have with the many other squadrons in the wing play an important dynamic in ensuring your unit succeeds in its mission. Few units can perform their mission in isolation; cooperation amongst squadrons is essential to success in the Air Force. Further, one of the commander's key actions is to oversee interactions with activities outside the unit, allowing squadron members the freedom to accomplish the mission internally. A sharp commander acts as a combination giant shield and absorbent sponge—reflecting, absorbing, and filtering external inputs to the squadron and enabling everyone else to go about their business.

Your Fellow Squadron Commanders

Once you've been able to meet most, if not all, of your squadron members, it's essential that you get out to introduce yourself to those group and wing officers who will play an important part in your command—your fellow squadron commanders. One of the first things that happens after you take the guidon of command is that your peer group changes dramatically. Simply put, you're no longer "one of the gang." Group commanders should not be left out either. The time you likely are first introduced to these wing leaders will occur at the post–change of command reception. Although this occurs in a social setting, it's important to follow this short introduction with a more formal one. Within days of your taking command—not weeks—set up a courtesy call with each of their offices. If you have the option, take a squadron coin, hat, or patch as a welcoming gesture. They'll remember you for it. Leave a business card if you have one. Ask them what you and your squadron can do for them. Flesh out what their specific needs are, how well (or not) things have gone in the past, and exchange ideas so your squadrons can be of mutual benefit to the overall team goal of the group and wing.

"One of the most important things I did just after assuming my commands was to get out and make appointments with my fellow squadron commanders as a way of introduction," said Lt Col Rollins Hickman. "It didn't have to be a long meeting, but it was a great opportunity to sit down, one on one, in their offices, and talk about where we were going together toward helping make the group and wing better accomplish its mission. I asked them what it is I and my squadron could do to help their squadron's individual mission. I took the time to let them know where I, too, thought their squadron could help my mission get accomplished," he added.[2] Colonel Hickman's excellent suggestion undoubtedly will pay big dividends down the road. As often is the case, soon after taking the guidon, you'll be swept up in the daily grind, and won't have the chance to talk with your fellow commanders outside of wing

---

Proverb for Leadership

A true leader is not satisfied with only knowing how to do what will get the organization through today; you must also be concerned about what it will need tomorrow. True leaders seek out opportunities; they're always looking for ways to increase their professional knowledge and skills.[3]

---

staff meetings, enlisted graduations, and other formal functions; nurture them as your allies and advocates early.

If you have a cadre of trusted confidants with whom you share personal, squadron, and sensitive issues, make sure you include a fellow squadron commander or two—particularly one who's been in command past the honeymoon or first quarter period. If you've chosen wisely, they will undoubtedly offer you insights that you may have missed and will often shed a different light on the situation.

As the new commander, you rarely will enter a situation where each unit commander totally agrees on every issue. Rather, there likely will be a lot of give and take on subjects that affect all squadrons. Also, natural rivalries are present in most wings. These rivalries may result from multiple units performing the same or similar missions, or squadrons with slightly different missions using the same equipment or competing for the same space or units borrowing or using personnel from other units. These rivalries or competitions can be healthy for the wing if the squadron commanders can maintain their focus on how to improve mission accomplishment. Be careful, though, for focusing on these rivalries can get ugly if the involved commanders start taking things personally and focus their squadron on doing better while simultaneously making the other units look bad—this accomplishes nothing.

All squadrons should enjoy some healthy rivalry, but be careful that it doesn't go too far and create professional walls

46

between units. Although this tactic may appear to have a short-term positive influence on you and your squadron, history is full of examples where this has failed miserably. Teamwork really does work, and the team is not restricted to your unit—all of the wing's elements work as a team.

The basic organization of some wings creates natural barriers to smooth squadron relationships totally. Two different commanders explained how one of their wing's squadrons trained personnel for three operational squadrons. The wing's dynamics led to a sometimes-adversarial relationship between the operational units and the training unit. The commanders eventually solved their squadron's long-existing differences but not without a good deal of compromise on each side. The main lesson was that the commanders were smart enough to place the wing's mission above squadron-only interests.

The key elements involved here were the squadron commanders themselves. They decided to work together first and then to allow their units to follow suit.

What are some of the things a peer group of squadron commanders can do to build a better team relationship? Here are a few examples.

1. Some wing commanders have been noted to take care of this issue directly by holding monthly wing/squadron commander luncheons. If such a program does not yet exist at your wing, take the lead and organize one. However, while this facilitated that particular relationship, it did not permit the squadron commanders to "hash it out" with each other as they sometimes needed periodic meetings of squadron commanders to discuss current issues, and topics are great facilitators of cross-feed information. As an option, get together for breakfast at the dining facility once a month or so without the wing/group commander.

2. More informal get-togethers work well also. And you don't have to have every other commander present to get some business done. Get together to jog together once a week or arrange to meet at the club every now and then to share ideas and gripes.

3. One commander explained to me how he and his fellow squadron commanders got together once a quarter to discuss personnel moves within the wing. If they all concurred on some proposed replacements, they would actively approach their boss with their unified suggestions.

4. Socialize together. Two or three times a year, the squadron commanders and their spouses might go out as a group, with nobody else going along. The commander who suggested it to me said it was pleasant going to a party where everyone there was on the same level—no one above or below you.

Your Boss

As with their peer group, most commanders interviewed enjoyed a good relationship with their bosses. In most cases, squadron commanders' bosses had themselves commanded squadrons before and understood many of the inherent challenges. They've been in your shoes. Also, bosses naturally want to see their commanders succeed; to a degree, their own success depends on their subordinate units' successful performance. Indeed, most group commanders will admit that they exist to facilitate optimum squadron operations—squadron commanders are truly the key leaders.

Many bosses or supervisors of squadron commanders will let the commander run the outfit as he or she sees fit; this type of situation is great. However, I've heard of a few bosses who tended to micromanage squadrons—if you get one like this, you may have to walk a tightrope to keep firm control. The micromanagers tend to micromanage only small segments of a squadron's operation—those areas they feel most comfortable with. The best advice I can offer here is to ascertain quickly what aspects of your unit are likely to get a lot of attention, become a subject matter expert in these hot areas, and do your best to shield your people in any hot area from undue scrutiny.

A number of squadron commanders mentioned that their immediate boss, usually a group commander, was not collocated on their base. Their geographical separation added another dimension to the relationship between the squadron and group commander. This can sometimes be a good thing or a bad thing if it is not handled properly. Lt Col James Weimer commanded the 763d Expeditionary Airlift Squadron (C-130) at Seeb North AB, Muscat, Oman. As head of an expeditionary unit supporting operations in Southwest Asia, the commander had the added burden of commanding his squadron with his group commander located hundreds of miles away at Prince Sultan AB, Saudi Arabia. "My boss and I talked every week at a certain, predetermined time. It was essentially a weekly staff meeting with me, and since we scheduled it well in advance, it allowed us to clear our schedules accordingly. Of course, if I needed his ear in between those times, I called him whenever I needed him. I never felt at a loss to talk to my boss,"[4] observed Colonel Weimer.

Finally, a new squadron commander will quickly realize that he serves more than one boss. The immediate supervisor is likely to be some kind of group commander. You also may have responsibilities to a major command or an Air Force-level directorate. However, the wing commander is also a boss—the big boss. Some wing commanders use different styles to run the show. Some will deal or interface solely with their group commanders and deputies; others will deal mostly with the deputies and some squadron commanders; and some others frequently will work directly with the squadron commanders. A squadron commander's job here is to find out how the game is being played in the wing and adjust to the new style. Be smart: if you backbrief your immediate supervisor when necessary, you should stay out of trouble. Also, it might be wise to get a handle on the relationship between your immediate boss and the wing commander. If they have complimentary personalities and share the same vision, things are relatively easy. If they don't, you may experience some problems. Be prepared.

Building Unit Cohesion and Morale

Morale makes up three quarters of the game, the relative balance of manpower accounts for only the remaining quarter.

—Napoleon

49

Building unit cohesion and morale may be one of your most challenging tasks. There is always a variety of things going on to drag down unit cohesion and morale, whether intentional or not. Even if you were lucky enough to inherit a squadron whose morale already was high, you can be assured it was so because your predecessor made it a top priority. And, keeping it high must be one of your top priorities as well.

Lt Col Eileen Isola offered, "I had to tackle a unit identity problem right off the bat. I made sure that every airman in the command knew what their purpose was in the squadron, what the unit mission was, and how very important their contribution was to making our mission a success."[5] Ensuring that every member of your squadron fully understands and embraces the mission of your unit is a cornerstone of unit cohesion. Every member must feel a purpose for his or her service. It's imperative that everyone is singing from the same sheet of music—and the commander is the orchestra's maestro.

Proverb for Command

To motivate your people, give them missions that challenge them. Give them as much responsibility as they can handle; then let them do the work without looking over their shoulders and nagging them. When they succeed, praise them. When they fall short, give them credit for what they have done and counsel or coach them on how to do better next time. People who are trained this way will accomplish the mission, even when no one is watching. They will work harder than they thought they could. And when their leader notices and gives them credit, they will be ready to take on even more next time.[6]

Added Lt Col Michael Prusz, who commanded the 343d Reconnaissance Squadron (RC-135), Offutt AFB, Nebraska, "Build an identity for your organization. An identity fosters improved esprit de corps. I have seen enhanced mission performance in an organization that held simple but effective farewell luncheons and handed out plaques. These luncheons reminded everyone of the unit's collective mission and desire to recognize people that continued to produce the unit's success."[7]

There are two significant reasons that building and maintaining high unit cohesion and morale are so difficult: there isn't a single checklist to make them happen, and there are so many variables to touch upon that it necessarily takes up a good portion of your time. What's good for the goose may not be good for the gander, and what one airman likes another may not like at all. This is not a case where "you can't be all things to all people," it's broader than that. Above all, what my experiences have shown and those corroborated by other squadron commanders have proven is this: lead by example.

You might be saying, "Lead by example? I've heard that statement so many times it's lost its significance." Maybe so, but I hope not. Assimilating all the many pieces of advice offered in this work is the true challenge for the new squadron commander. This is the most important time to "walk the walk, and talk the talk." Referring to the adage of the glass house, your troops are constantly watching you. If you appear to be having fun, they'll have little reason not to have fun as well. If you appear to be taking the unit's mission seriously, they will, too. If you appear to work hard and play hard, they'll follow your lead in trail.

Proverb for Leadership

There are no cookie-cutter solutions to leadership challenges, and there are no shortcuts to success. However, the tools are available to every leader. It is up to you to master and use them.[8]

"One thing I instituted to build unit cohesion that worked well for me early in my command that probably doesn't come to many people's minds was to have an occasional open ranks inspection," said Lt Col Don Flowers, who commanded the 66th Logistics Squadron, Hanscom AFB, Massachusetts. "I know it doesn't sound like a crowd pleaser, and it wasn't at first, but it kept everyone in line and reminded them that they were in the Air Force. Everyone was treated equally and fairly, and it stopped complacency. The standards were high. Those who were exceptional were given letters of excellence and 24-hour passes as appropriate. Morale quickly increased," he added.[9]

Maj Jay Carroll had an interesting idea that helped spark his unit's morale. For such a large unit, and one that needed constant care and feeding, he came up with a good morale-boosting idea for his security forces squadron. "I knew I had some of the Air Force's sharpest people working for me and the wing, yet they didn't look that way. We had elite, handpicked airmen working the gates, but didn't have the proper uniforms for them. So I asked my boss for additional funds for special uniforms and equipment for our elite gate guards. They felt proud and distinguished. It paid huge dividends."[10]

The many successes of former squadron commanders who have offered advice will be captured in this section as well as in specific portions of chapter 3 under "People."

On-Duty Cohesion and Morale

Col Mark Browne had a significant challenge of rebuilding his squadron into a cohesive team of recruiters. He commanded more than 100 personnel who were spread over nearly 500 square miles in the rural areas of Louisiana, Arkansas, and Mississippi. He went back to the basics of leadership. He clearly understood where the squadron needed to be with respect to unit cohesion and morale, and he successfully articulated his vision to the entire squadron of where he wanted the squadron to end up in one year. He brought his senior noncommissioned officer corps on board, and with their buy-in, he set out to travel among his command to meet each member and discuss his vision. "This is something that I quickly noticed was missing. The recruiters were so engrossed in meeting their specific recruiting goals that they lost sight of the big picture. I thought it was my responsibility to get them back on track."[11]

The morale of your squadron's personnel comes from three sources: a feeling that they have an important job to do, a feeling that they are trained to do it well, and a feeling that their great work is appreciated and recognized. Of course, it is the commander who inculcates these ideals.

Lt Col George Eichelberger inherited a healthy squadron when he took command of the 390th Intelligence Squadron, Kadena AB, Japan. He recognized that although morale seemed to be at a pretty high level, it wouldn't stay that way long without keeping the flame lit. "Keeping morale up wasn't that difficult. It took some effort on my part to act as the squadron cheerleader all the time, and it helped when I kept reminding each of my squadron members how important they were to the mission of the squadron. Even though we didn't have a nine-to-five mentality, it was tough sometimes to keep everyone focused, and I felt it was my responsibility to set and maintain the vision."[12]

Lt Col Donald Flowers had an interesting approach to maintaining unit cohesion. He recalled, "While up in Massachusetts, one of our airmen suggested we help keep the areas outside the base clean by picking up trash every quarter or so. I thought it was a great idea (that was supported by the whole squadron), so we signed up with the state as part of the Adopt a Highway program. It was great!"[13]

Finally, the leader must constantly walk the fine line between focusing on the immediate task and focusing on group cohesion. The work of strategic decision making is tedious, difficult, and tension-provoking. Without tension, the work will not proceed. With too much tension, the group will focus on the tension itself rather than on the work to be done. One of the leader's many jobs is to maintain this delicate balance, to jointly optimize progress and group health.

Off-Duty Cohesion and Morale

Off-duty time is also extremely important to you and your personnel, whether it's an informal gathering after work, a squadron intramural sporting event, or a baby shower. Therefore, it's something that will require your attention.

Once again, many commanders handled this situation completely differently from others, citing their base location as the most common driving factor. Those who commanded at remote or rural locations (i.e., Osan AB, Korea; Minot AFB, North Dakota; or Laughlin AFB, Texas) enjoyed closer squadron relations, both on and off duty. Because there simply wasn't a great deal of activities available in the local community, it necessarily forced them to socialize as a group outside the unit. Every commander interviewed who commanded a squadron in one of these areas remarked how much he or she enjoyed this particular aspect of their tenure in command.

Conversely, those who have commanded in urban areas (i.e., Nellis AFB, Nevada; Hickam AFB, Hawaii; or Stuttgart AB, Germany) found that their unit's personnel often did not want to pursue an active squadron-centered social life outside the squadron. There were plenty of activities to be found within the local community. These commanders remarked that this, too, was not a problem for them.

Both examples highlight the fact that building unit cohesion and morale off duty is not absolutely necessary, but it is an option for the commander if he or she sees the need. Bottom line: feel the pulse of the squadron and don't force it.

Formal Inspections

If you don't have enough responsibilities on your plate by now, the Air Force is always willing to add a few more. If you are commanding an Air Force squadron, the chances are high that you'll have at least one formal inspection like a Unit Compliance Inspection (UCI), Operational Readiness Inspection (ORI), or Standardization and Evaluation visit. This is not only an important evaluation of your squadron—it's a direct evaluation of you and your leadership. Few, if any, inspections are truly no-notice evaluations, so you should have ample time to prepare your squadron accordingly. Said Lt Col Robert Suminsby Jr., "Formal inspections are the only chance you get, outside combat, to *prove* how good you are."

Before the Inspection

What have others done in this situation? The first place to start is with the past inspection results. What areas did the inspectors evaluate? How well did your squadron do during the last inspection? How long has it been since the last formal visit? You may have to start your planning from scratch, particularly if your unit has had a heavy turnover of personnel. Do you know what agency is scheduled to give the inspection? You probably do. Call the functional managers of the inspection team and open up a dialogue with them. They'll likely give you a good vector as to what they're going to be looking at during their visit, and this too will help you build a plan for your squadron.

How far in advance you begin your planning and preparation will be completely up to you, given the circumstances and scope of the visit. You undoubtedly will have something already on your plate, given the operations tempo and personnel tempo of your unit, so prioritizing will be especially important. Although you do not operate in a vacuum, it is definitely your responsibility to chart the course for your squadron. Your planning must begin first, and when you have an idea of how you want to attack the subject, write it down on paper—and then put it away for a week or so. Revisit the plan after you've had some time to think of your strategy, and then do the next most important thing—put the right person in charge of executing your vision.

Like anything else, having the right person in the right job usually ends with great success. For their success and yours, do your very best to clear as many extraneous tasks off their plate as possible to give them the time they need to prepare adequately. Give them the tools and resources necessary to do their job well. Perhaps most importantly, keeping them, as well as yourself, motivated will help keep you all focused and on track.

Prepping too far in advance can be as much a problem as prepping too late. The tried and tested law of "burnout" may apply. Be careful not to peak too early.

Former commanders tell me that the type of inspection and the inspection philosophy of the major command are two important factors to consider when preparing a unit. One of the easiest ways to prepare for an inspection is simply to read the mail, beginning with past squadron and wing inspection reports. Any problem areas identified in the past definitely will be closely scrutinized again. Your squadron also should receive the results of other wings' inspections by the same inspection team that is going to visit you. Pay attention to what these reports say, and you will have a blueprint of what the inspection team is currently emphasizing.

Most commanders stress the need for a solid self-inspection program. One officer told me that he actively used a year-round program to constantly fine-tune his unit's mission and programs. Major inspections then normally fell in line with existing self-inspection efforts, and erratic or extraordinary preparation efforts were not necessary. Many commanders used this type of approach and involved all unit personnel, emphasizing that the squadron would succeed or fail together.

Other commanders related that routine, year-round self-inspection programs are better in theory than in practice. They would appoint a small team of experienced supervisors to specifically run through the entire squadron self-inspection program a couple of months before the inspection to identify potential problem areas. Timing is crucial; self-inspections shouldn't wait until the last minute. They necessitate solid documentation, and above all else, demand an honest, close look at squadron performance.

During the Inspection

Clearly, your primary concern here is to remain focused. Keep focused on the task at hand, and do your best to ensure everyone else keeps the same focus.

The specific actions you take in leading and guiding your squadron to success will largely depend on what type of inspection you are receiving. Once the inspection team arrives, you and others probably will be relieved to get the inspection under way and finished. After their departure, tuck your winning results away for the next "lucky" commander who gets the next chance to excel. As always, your leadership will play a big part in your squadron's success during an inspection, and most former commanders will tell you to take the lead early and literally lead the way.

A former flying squadron commander related that he thought it was absolutely necessary to be the one to take the first in-flight evaluation on the toughest mission. When you step back and think about this tactic, it makes good sense for several reasons. First, his squadron personnel will respect the commander's close involvement in the inspection by putting himself in the line of fire first. Lead by example. Second, he considered it would get his unit off on the right track because he thought it critical to be the best in the weapon system and, as such, would set the stage for the following evaluations. And finally, he knew that any inspection team would more closely investigate a squadron whose commander tried to duck the schedule during a formal inspection.

Like any inspection, whether it's a normal squadron visit from the wing commander (if that can be called normal) or a full-blown major command (MAJCOM) inspection, you'll want to make sure the red carpet is put out. Continue to keep your unit clean and free of debris (a dirty and unkempt squadron sends a poor message). Keep enough moles around, in addition to yourself, to make sure that any minor infraction uncovered by the team on one day doesn't happen the next. Get the word out to your troops—the inspectors will be impressed and notice that you've made attempts to correct the infractions on the spot and prevent any repeats.

If you're fortunate enough to have a sister squadron of like mission or function that may be getting inspected before your unit does, you should capitalize on being a great fellow squadron commander. Without crossing any ethical boundaries, keep a close eye on the progress of their inspection and make changes in your unit as necessary.

Four general areas of advice came from the group interviewed most often. They were as follows:

1. Be smart and put your best foot forward.
2. Be positive, honest, and aboveboard.
3. Put your personal expertise and leadership to work.
4. Stay informed during the inspection.

Some inspection teams will want or need specific information either before they arrive or very shortly after they get to your base. Be smart and provide them everything they want when they want it. If there are certain portions of this information you are particularly proud of and want to emphasize, make sure you highlight it. One squadron commander described a new squadron program that had just been completed before the team's arrival. It was the first such program in the command, and it dealt directly with the unit's mission. He went out of his way to emphasize this new program, and the inspection team was clearly impressed. In fact, the team spent so much time looking at his program (in an effort to benchmark it commandwide) that they didn't have as much time left to scrutinize some other programs that may not have been as good. And if you weren't the principal architect of that particular award-winning program, make sure the inspector knows the names of those who were to give them the recognition they deserve.

Another facet of being smart concerns your scheduling plans during the inspection. The inspection team will be looking to make sure you haven't allowed your weakest team members to take leave during the inspection, and they may ask to see a unit personnel roster to verify those personnel who were not present due to a temporary-duty tasking. While you shouldn't encourage your weakest folks to take leave during the formal inspection, and in many cases you won't have complete control of short-notice temporary-duty taskings, you also shouldn't put your newest and most inexperienced people on the toughest shifts or during known periods of difficult inspections. You wouldn't schedule that way in war if you could avoid it, so don't do it here, either. A balanced schedule of your unit's personnel, ensuring the most experienced are teamed with the least experienced, works well in most situations.

If the inspector general (or any other type of inspection team) finds some obvious problems during the inspection, don't spend a lot of time (if any) trying to talk your way out of it unless the team is actually wrong and their call will affect other portions of your unit's inspection. For example, if an inspector finds some minor administrative discrepancies with your squadron's leave program, acknowledge the errors, ask for advice on how to improve the program, and move on. Get over it. Don't let a few minor things snowball into the major portion of the inspection. Most commanders who have been through an inspection will agree that being honest and up front was the best advice to follow. Generally speaking, the inspectors themselves are experts in the areas they are looking hard at and won't be fooled easily. You should cut your losses by acknowledging a problem area, fix it as quickly as possible, and press on to more important matters at hand.

After the Inspection

Although you may be relieved to see the inspection completed, there's still a bit of work to do before you get to celebrate. For example, you should document every finding you can in some type of after action report. This serves many purposes, not the least of which is to fix any problems unearthed by the inspection team. There's generally no better time than the present in these situations to mend any broken fences. Although your unit personnel may be tired and not happy about it, fixing these problem areas while the griddle's hot is always better than trying to do it later. Following this advice means events will be fresh on yours and their minds, and you'll likely have all the primary players in place to get it done more quickly and efficiently.

A good technique is to give your troops a day of rest to catch their breath and allow them to collect their thoughts. Have your senior leadership hold a series of meetings to gather the pertinent data from each of your squadron's individual shops or flights. Then host a single meeting with just the key players where you can lead the debrief for the entire unit. This type of internal squadron cross-feed enables unit personnel to see the bigger picture and allows everyone to get on the same page to benefit from the team's observations. Inspectors will often pass on some valuable information or techniques used by other MAJCOM units that you can pass on to the entire squadron when appropriate to improve the unit's overall mission capability. Don't miss this golden opportunity.

Another good reason to hold an after action review is to capture those lessons learned for future inspections. This was considered vital by many squadron commanders. One officer related that he kept a detailed log of events as he saw them, included them with the informal after action review notes, and filed them away for the next commander. The golden rule seems always to work.

I took advantage of holding these same review meetings after a particularly successful ORI. In addition to the above-mentioned advantages, I found my notes to be extremely useful during the rest of the year when I had to write and edit both officer and enlisted performance reports. You may not have the luxury of having a unit historian of any type, so it's up to you to take care of the troops by keeping track of your past successes. I had to return several performance reports for a rewrite because those who wrote them failed to include such pertinent information. These notes also will come in handy if you are fortunate enough to have your squadron submitted for any United States Air Force, MAJCOM, or wing-level annual awards. Doing a little bit of work now will pay big dividends later.

Now it's time to party! Assuming the inspection went well, it is very appropriate to have some type of social gathering to thank those who participated and to recognize those who excelled. This could be something as simple as a backyard burger burn or a full-blown party at your squadron or club. Having some type of celebration, regardless of the inspection's outcome, brings closure to the hard work your unit's members (and their families) have put in over the last several months. It provides a healthy breather before getting back to work on the next task.

Recall again the leadership lessons of Colonel Chamberlain's victory at Little Round Top. He focused on the mission and objective, established a strategy based on known information, maintained the fluidity to adapt to a rapidly changing battlefield, and above all, led his troops with confidence even in the face of the many unknowns. There were no black-and-white checklists to leadership in his situation; and I emphasize the same for you, the new squadron commander. But there were distinct guiding principles for mission accomplishment, and those will buttress your command just as they did Chamberlain's.

Notes

1. Col John G. Meyer Jr., *Company Command—The Bottom Line* (Washington, D.C.: National Defense University Press, 1990), 30.

2. Lt Col Rollins Hickman, interviewed by author, Maxwell Air Force Base (AFB), Ala., 16 November 2001.

3. Army Field Manual (FM) 22-100, *Army Leadership*, 31 August 1999.

4. Lt Col James Weimer, interviewed by author, Maxwell AFB, Ala., 14 November 2001.

5. Lt Col Eileen Isola, interviewed by author, Maxwell AFB, Ala., 5 September 2001.

6. FM 22-100.

7. Lt Col Michael Prusz, telephone interview with author, Offutt AFB, Nebr., 27 February 2002.

8. FM 22-100.

9. Lt Col Donald Flowers, interviewed by author, Maxwell AFB, Ala., 6 December 2001.

10. Maj Jay Carroll, interviewed by author, Maxwell AFB, Ala., 13 February 2002.

11. Col Mark Browne, interviewed by author, Maxwell AFB, Ala., 4 September 2001.

12. Lt Col George Eichelberger, interviewed by author, Maxwell AFB, Ala., 5 September 2001.

13. Flowers interview.

Chapter 3

People

This chapter is the longest because it is the most important. If you read nothing else, pay attention to the great advice offered here by successful squadron commanders.

While it seems that *everything* is important to the squadron commander—and most things are—*nothing* is as important, vital, and critical to you, the commander, as your unit's personnel. They are truly your bread and butter, without which the mission simply could not be completed. Spend as much time with your troops as possible. You (and they) will love it.

> *If you want to manage something, manage yourself. Do that well, and you'll be ready to stop managing—and start leading.*
>
> —Source Unknown

Welcome

The size and scope of your squadron likely will determine the amount of time you devote to meeting all squadron newcomers formally. You may command a squadron with a very high operations tempo (OPTEMPO) rate where either you or your troops are serving temporary duty (TDY) or one with non-collocated detachments or flights where you must travel to visit them. Regardless, it is wise to make every attempt to meet with as many people as you can, as soon as you can. Several commanders held a Right-Start type meeting monthly to speak with every new member. Others ensured that all senior non-commissioned and commissioned officers met with them in a one-on-one session in the commander's office for 15 to 20 minutes each session. With a large squadron, this may take some time, but it will be well spent.

Newcomer Inbriefings

The overall advice gleaned from former squadron commanders is that you must meet with your new folks in any way that is comfortable to you and fits your schedule. The fact that you may command a 24-hour squadron with shift workers, for example, will play an obvious role in where and when you can meet with your assigned personnel.

"I met with every member of my squadron when they arrived here," said Lt Col Michael Retallick, who commanded the 21st Airlift Squadron (C-5) at Travis AFB, California. "It was a challenge, particularly given the very high OPTEMPO rate of my C-5 unit, but I had a great secretary who managed to clear my schedule every ten days or so for me to meet the folks who had just arrived through a permanent change of station. I think it's extremely important to set the stage right away with a good first impression. I took the opportunity not just to welcome the new member but to ask how their family was doing and whether there was anything I could do for them. First impressions last a lifetime," he continued.[1]

Most commanders set the stage for the squadron's new arrivals by ensuring a robust sponsor program was firmly in place and entrenched in the unit's standards for all those new personnel assigned to the squadron. Your orderly room personnel likely will be the ones first notified of all inbound personnel. Armed with this information, you should assign someone to sponsor the new person. Do they need training? If this is their first time acting as a sponsor, ensure they have your vision on how the squadron sponsor program should work. Generally, it is best if you assign a person who is from the same shop or flight, one close in rank, and one who will be with your unit for the next several months to ensure continuity. This allows for a more personal touch (and classy one) that will signal the new arrival that he or she is coming to an excellent Air Force squadron.

Once the sponsor has been designated, he or she should personally contact the person by telephone or electronically (by E-mail), as a minimum, to welcome the inbound to the squadron. Without question, ensure you include a personal welcome letter. Once you've written the master letter, it'll be much easier to simply personalize each letter thereafter. This makes a great first impression. Most commanders had a standard packet of information for the inbound troop. Going the extra step to personalize the welcoming packet adds a degree of professionalism, such as including a list of local schools (if they have children), day care centers (if they have infants or toddlers), places of worship, community arts or sports programs, and the like. They will be hungry for information, and it's your responsibility to ensure that the information is readily available. The wing's Family Support Center, Public Affairs office, and library will have appropriate information to include in the package, including base map, wing telephone directory, and general services information. Include a copy of the most recent wing newspaper and local newspaper also. Are they interested in real estate downtown? Include a copy of the local real estate listings from the base housing office. Send along a couple of wing and squadron patches should they wish to arrive with the proper uniform already sewn for duty. They'll definitely appreciate your efforts.

After a week or so has passed, ensure the assigned sponsor follows up the welcome packet with a personal telephone call. This will have given the new person some time to digest the information you've sent and allow him or her to ask some inevitable questions of the sponsor and your squadron commander. Gather some current information. What day and time will the new person arrive? Will he or she be traveling by auto or flying in by airplane? Will the individual need to be picked up at the airport, will he or she need billeting reservations, or does he or she have any special needs the sponsor can help with? It will take much less time for the sponsor to handle any such details than it would for the new arrival, and most importantly, it sets the right tone for your squadron.

Air Force members who receive this type of personal and caring treatment upon their arrival most likely will be extremely impressed and will do everything they can to support you and your squadron. Lt Col Robert Suminsby commanded overseas and had this perspective: "Such a personalized welcome program is particularly essential to a squadron located overseas. This may be the first time your troop has ever traveled outside the United States. The difficult language barriers, unusual traffic signs, and complex currency exchanges can be daunting for many people. Not only is meeting them (at the airport) a courtesy thing to do, it is sometimes essential. It sends a powerful message that you're there to support them."[2] Such a welcome program will instantly bond the new member and his or her family to your squadron and can't do anything other than enhance your unit's mission effectiveness.

Equally important is that you spend some time, even a few minutes, with those under your command who are leaving your unit (see more under "Your Exit Strategy," chapter 7). If you create an open and honest conversation in the feedback session, the advice you will get from those leaving your command may be the most valuable of all. In fact, including this step on your squadron's out-processing checklist is a good idea. Said Lt Col Alan Hunt, "I made every effort to spend a few private moments with those who were leaving my squadron to get some honest feedback. You'd be amazed what kind of frank feedback you can get from those departing!"[3]

Lt Col Matthew Black, who commanded the 84th Test and Evaluation Squadron at Tyndall AFB, Florida, also made it a special point to do the same for those who were departing the squadron, either through a PCS or retirement, as much as he did for those just arriving. "I asked for some honest feedback from those who were departing the unit. I realized that their focus was probably different than mine, and I knew that it was possible that I might have missed something, and wanted them to feel free to tell me about it. Feedback from those departing can be interesting,"[4] said Colonel Black.

Key Personnel

Unfortunately, not every squadron has the luxury of having a civilian secretary. However, since most do, or at least take an airman out of hide from the orderly room, there's some great advice to be offered from recently graduated squadron commanders on how to run your personal administration.

Your Secretary

"One of the most important things your secretary can do for you is to take control of your schedule. He or she must be empowered to schedule your week as you both see fit, and be allowed to be the gatekeeper to your day,"[5] advised Lt Col Terry Kono. He, like many other squadron commanders, echoed the importance of a good secretary. Unlike many people in an average Air Force squadron, your secretary can have a significant impact on the success of your squadron.

Not all secretaries are created equally, and in most cases, the squadron secretary is a civilian government employee who has been in the position for some time. Although your squadron secretary works for you as the commander, it is very wise for you to sit down with him or her early on in your command (the first week, for sure) to discuss how the secretary wants to run the office. It's likely that the secretary is well aware of how your group and wing administrations are run; therefore, there should be no need for you to reinvent the wheel.

As alluded to throughout this book, getting control of your schedule is imperative to your success. Whether you want to schedule a certain period of time daily to exercise or have a controlled 30 minutes a week for telephoning the spouses of your deployed personnel, make sure your secretary schedules the appropriate time—and stick to it! Your day can quickly get wasted away if you don't hold to a disciplined schedule. This is good advice to heed. "My schedule was gospel," said Lt Col Anthony Rock, who commanded the 95th Fighter Training Squadron (F-15C), Tyndall AFB, Florida. "I thought it important to periodically call the spouses of those deployed from my unit, just to see how they were doing and to ask if there was anything I could do for them. Calling them made a tremendous difference for the family to know that the commander cared, but I couldn't have done something like this if time hadn't been purposely blocked to do so."[6]

Some commanders suggested there were times when a secretary thought he or she *was* the commander, and all agreed that this was something that had to be corrected immediately. In their earnest zeal to control your schedule, some secretaries, who act as gatekeeper and stand as door guard, may carry their position too far. Because your secretary guards your schedule, screens telephone calls, and is the last person in your line of defense who controls who gets on your calendar, the opportunity to succumb to the power of the office can sometimes be overwhelming. One commander had this happen to him early in his tenure of command and decided to redefine the secretary's role. He said he was polite and up front about how he wanted things run in the command section, and she took it well and changed her practices.

No matter how well led your squadron is or how high morale is, "if the paperwork ain't right, it ain't right," said one commander. Again, depending on the specific duties you task your secretary with, he or she is often the last link for correcting and editing any paperwork that leaves your squadron. Many secretaries are used as a final check for performance reports, squadron awards and decorations, letters to parents and spouses, and the like. Every commander would like any such correspondence to leave the squadron in perfect order. Your secretary must be empowered to do so.

If you have given your secretary the authority and responsibility of such critical activities, it might be wise for you to mention the importance of his or her role to your squadron's senior staff or even to your entire unit as a whole at a commander's call. You may know what role the secretary plays, but others in your squadron may not, so it's important to ensure everyone is on the same page regarding squadron administration. If there's any one person in your unit that you need to keep happy and productive, it's your secretary!

Your Section Commander

While you may have the luxury of a secretary, you may not be afforded a full-time section commander. This position is usually reserved for the larger squadrons (typically squadrons with more than 350 personnel). A section commander is usually a "personnelist" and is usually a lieutenant or junior captain. If you don't have a formal section commander assigned to your unit, jump to the next section ("Your First Sergeant" in this chapter). If you do, read on for some good insight into the possibilities that exist here to aid you during your tenure in command.

As the term *commander* implies, your section commander has the opportunity to be placed on G-series orders (allowing him or her Uniform Code of Military Justice [UCMJ] authority, amongst other responsibilities). I say "opportunity" for command authority because only you, as the squadron commander, can authorize G-series orders to be published.

Whether or not you allow your section commander that authority needs to be carefully thought out. My succinct advice is this: make your decision based on experience, maturity, and level of responsibility. Often a junior officer doesn't yet possess these attributes, and you will probably not want to put him or her on orders. You may hold off a year or so to see what the individual's potential is and then allow him or her the opportunity to make lower-level, lesser-impacting decisions under your close watch until you feel more comfortable. Or, if you are as fortunate as I was during my command, you may have a lieutenant who was prior enlisted, is older, and displays tremendous maturity. I authorized my section commander G-series authority shortly after taking command. He was that good.

As you will soon find out, your signature will become a hot commodity after taking the guidon. In addition, depending on the size of your squadron, you'll have scores of official documents, correspondence, performance reports, reenlistments, and retirement paperwork to sign almost immediately. Protect your signature. Your section commander, given the proper authority from you, can aid you immeasurably in this arena. Much paperwork is routine and therefore doesn't have to have your particular attention other than the fact that the squadron commander is responsible to sign it. As mentioned in chapter 1, most new commanders feel that they need to see everything for the first few months to get a grasp of what's going on in the unit. Soon you will want to wean yourself from the need to be in the weeds and will enjoy handing that responsibility off to your section commander. It can be a great help to you, particularly with time-management concerns.

The touchier area with respect to your unit's section commander is whether you should allow him or her to handle UCMJ administrative punishment. Again, you can limit authority to lower-level action, or you can grant full access to the range of possibilities authorized a commander, commensurate with their rank. Realize that the range of punishment a captain can levy is less than that of a lieutenant colonel. Most former squadron commanders interviewed did not allow that authority, citing lack of experience and maturity as the driving factors. A few granted limited access not only to help ease their workload (considering large squadrons) but as a means of mentoring their section commander. Keen oversight is mandatory here. Doling out authority in these instances can be a terrific method of challenging the officer's professional growth. And, as is true in many other things in the early stages, it will actually take you more time to train the individual than it would for you to do it yourself. This is just another role for you as the squadron commander!

Your First Sergeant

You may not know it yet, but your first sergeant clearly can make or break your squadron from every vantage. You may be the squadron's *formal* leader, but he or she, not you, is the most important *informal* leader of your squadron. In addition, as such, this area deserves a great deal of attention. I've elected to use the framework of Col John G. Meyer's book, *Company Command—The Bottom Line*, to discuss the important role of the first sergeant and his or her relationship to the commander.

Day One with Your First Sergeant. The most important meeting with your first sergeant is the first one immediately after you assume command. Here, the two of you will establish the plan to command and run your squadron. Having this meeting soon after the change of command sends a powerful signal to the unit on the importance of the commander/first sergeant relationship. Give your Shirt a week's notice about the meeting. Explain your agenda and ask him or her to be ready to discuss what the squadron's goals should be and other matters you consider important. Schedule a firm time and permit no outside interruptions. Try to accomplish the following:

1. Get the first sergeant's ideas on command philosophy.
2. Develop and agree on unit goals, standards, and objectives. Specify and publish them. You and your first

sergeant must be on the same priority frequency to ensure fairness across the board.

3. Discuss your expectations of a first sergeant. You may not have any experience with a first sergeant yet; to develop expectations, you'll need to talk to other squadron commanders, or your group commander, for advice.

4. Seek the first sergeant's expectations of you.

5. Emphasize open, two-way communication. For example, guarantee the first sergeant his or her day in court.

6. Determine the first sergeant's role in UCMJ and administrative separation procedures. For example, the first sergeant should advise, recommend, initiate, check (to ensure you have all details and supporting documents to make a fair and just decision), protect your airman's rights, and supervise any punishment imposed.

7. Define a general division of labor. You should have a division of labor because neither of you can do everything yourself. You and your first sergeant must agree on what areas each will emphasize and then keep each other totally informed. You alone are responsible for what goes on in the squadron; however, you can better accomplish the mission if you and your first sergeant share the workload.

The number one responsibility of any first sergeant is to ensure that the health, morale, welfare, and discipline of the squadron are the best they can be. He or she must have your confidence to do so, and you, in turn, must give him or her the full range of authority you can muster.

You may think your highest ranking SNCO or chief is your conduit to the enlisted corps but that is not so—it's your first sergeant who carries that banner. That is not to say that his or her position violates the formal chain of command, but the "Shirt" is your link to the entire squadron, especially the enlisted personnel. Your first sergeant plays many roles in your squadron, wears many hats, and carries many issues forward for you and for your review.

Every commander interviewed agreed that the effectiveness of the first sergeant, and his or her relationship to the squadrons, is critical to morale and function. Without question, the relationship between your first sergeant and you as the commander is essential to any success. "Within 30 minutes of taking the guidon I had my first closed door meeting with my First Sergeant. We shared each other's vision and goals. And then I stepped out of the office with him by my side. Every member of the squadron knew the First Sergeant had my complete trust and confidence, which came in handy later down the road,"[7] said Lt Col Kurt Klausner.

SMSgt Walter Lilley Jr., an instructor at the USAF First Sergeant Academy, Maxwell AFB, Alabama, offered this perspective: "The relationship between the commander and his First Sergeant is perhaps the most critical relationship in the squadron—it has to be. It's almost like a marriage between the two. The First Sergeant must understand and share the commander's vision for the squadron and he must embrace it with fervor. And the commander must trust the First Sergeant and give him the authority and responsibility he needs to carry out his many responsibilities."[8]

Lt Col Dennis Jones commanded the 551st Special Operations Squadron (MH-53), Kirtland AFB, New Mexico. A large squadron (more than 300) consisting of personnel in rank from airman basic to major, and in age from 18 to 40, gave a new appreciation for the first sergeant and the significance of his leadership at the squadron level. "My First Sergeant was the best thing that ever happened to the 551st. We had an MH-53 flying training mission, with a portion of the squadron changing faces every couple of months. He was the glue that kept it all together,"[9] remembered Colonel Jones. He also stressed the importance of having the right commander-first sergeant bond for things to go well, for without it, things could sour quickly: "Our relationship 'clicked' right away, which is the way it needs to be. If things aren't working out between you and the Shirt, then either fix it immediately or find a new First Sergeant. It was up to me to clearly identify my vision of where I wanted the squadron to go, and to make sure the Shirt not only understood me, but was on the same sheet of music. He was, and our squadron did very well."[10]

Unfortunately, not all squadron commander-first sergeant relationships work out for the betterment of the squadron—or each other. As I write this, there is a severe shortage of diamond-wearing first sergeants throughout the Air Force, and the trend isn't showing relief any time soon. As such, your unit may have to take a SNCO (usually a master sergeant) out of hide to have him act as your first sergeant. He is commonly referred to as an "Undershirt" (see "Undershirt" in this chapter) or additional duty first sergeant. The Air Force doesn't have a problem with this notion, but you must realize that the person you select won't have had the formal training normally given to First Sergeant Academy graduates. This omission can be critical, particularly when dealing with sensitive disciplinary issues. Heavy oversight from the wing judge advocate's office will likely be necessary, especially if he or she is expected to handle any formal nonjudicial punishment. Encourage him or her to run any such issue through another diamond-wearing first sergeant assigned to your group or wing.

What do you do when you can't get along with your first sergeant? This can be touchy, but as you'll read in more detail in chapter 4, being up front and deadly honest is the only path to take regarding this issue. Because there is no abundance of first sergeants available in most wings, the old days of being able to interview several candidates to match your personalities and squadron vision are gone for the near future. You essentially get what you're given. Similarly, diamond wearers normally screen potential first sergeant candidates closely during shadow programs. It truly is a select Air Force Specialty Code (AFSC).

In the majority of USAF wings today, the overall responsibility of wing first sergeant manning and squadron placement falls under the wing's command chief master sergeant. He or she does the best he can to shuffle the first sergeants to a different squadron every year or so for a variety of reasons: their experience and growth, an occasional personality clash between a commander and the Shirt, a first sergeant promotion offering the greater responsibilities of a larger squadron, new first sergeant acquisition, Shirt PCS moves, and the like. Consult with your command chief on these issues.

Again, what do you do if you have a personality clash with your first sergeant? What if you and your shirt don't see eye to eye on key issues? What if the first sergeant doesn't share your vision for the squadron? There are several options. Here is a couple of ideas offered by a few squadron commanders who faced such a situation:

1. Be brutally honest about your concerns. The first sergeant deserves the truth, and you must not be shy in talking about it.

2. Try to win him or her over. The first sergeant will go through many more commanders during his or her tenure than you will. The more experienced shirts will know how to refocus their priorities if you give them the chance.

3. Look in the mirror. Are you the one causing the friction? Confide in your secretary, section commander, or executive officer (someone who has witnessed you together). It's entirely possible that you don't see a personal weakness that can easily be corrected if known.

4. Ask your boss or fellow squadron commanders for advice. They've all been in your position and may have great words for you.

5. Fire him when all else fails. Visit the command chief master sergeant immediately to have him or her either replaced as soon as possible, or go without one if you have to.

The one area that all commanders and first sergeants interviewed agreed on was this: a bad relationship between the commander and his first sergeant is much, much worse than having no first sergeant at all. It's not good for you; it's not good for the Shirt; and it's definitely not good for your squadron. As one commander put it, "Make every attempt to rectify the situation quickly and if it still doesn't work out, cut the umbilical cord, now!"

The first sergeant literally is available 24/7 to take care of your squadron's personnel. As a matter of experience, his or her time *away* from the squadron working issues on your behalf may exceed the time spent *in* the squadron. This can easily cause burnout in even the most energetic first sergeant.

Remember that as a squadron commander, your command tour usually will last two years, something you can sprint through. But your first sergeant likely will have spent a couple of years wearing the diamond before your arrival and will stay on for another several years. The first sergeant must learn to pace himself or herself, and your responsibility as the commander is to ensure the first sergeant does this.

Taking Care of Your First Sergeant. The first sergeant is responsible for taking care of everyone in your unit, so whose responsibility is it to take care of your first sergeant? Without question, it's *your* responsibility! It is easy to forget to take care of those closest to you while you spend a great deal of effort taking care of others. As such, your first sergeant often falls off the radar scope. Take time daily to sit down behind closed doors, with no outside interference, and talk with your Shirt. Schedule it. Stick to the schedule. The mentoring that each of you receives from one another will prove extremely valuable day in and day out.

Many commanders interviewed admitted that this area was one of their weakest during their commands. Ask some helpful questions: How is his or her family? When is he or she going to take some time off? Does he or she need a break? What about his or her professional career? Has he completed any Community College of the Air Force (CCAF) advanced academic courses or appropriate professional military education (PME) courses, and so on? All admitted that in their efforts to sprint through their command tours, they failed to recognize the first sergeant needed to be on a steadier pace to avoid supernova burnout.

A standard practice most squadron commanders used to help mitigate the first sergeant's burnout was to personally take the Shirt's phone and responsibilities from him or her every other weekend or so, or, better yet, to seek others in the squadron to volunteer to do so. Your section commander or any of your other SNCOs throughout the unit may be a good substitute. Try to make this a standard practice. It not only gives your Shirt a much-needed break, but it also allows other SNCOs the opportunity to take on added responsibilities, get

75

a taste of first sergeant duties, and have the opportunity to interface directly with you as the commander.

Undershirt. You may be aware that for a first sergeant to earn his or her coveted diamond, he or she must first attend a formal training course. Open to all SNCOs (master sergeant and above), an interested individual must first volunteer. Once selected by the wing's leadership, he or she will then attend a formal four-week training course at the USAF First Sergeant Academy (USAF FSA) located at Maxwell AFB, Alabama. The candidates participate in rigorous academic training covering a variety of subjects before earning the diamond. Then he or she will be authorized to wear the diamond while assigned to first sergeant duties.

However, you may not be aware of an informal program for SNCOs who volunteer to act as a first sergeant for a squadron without one or act as an undershirt to augment a squadron's first sergeant for a squadron large enough to need one. Regardless of the size of the squadron, you may want to consider the Undershirt option to spread the first sergeant's duties to another individual on occasion to take care of your Shirt. This program is also an excellent one to help recruit sharp SNCOs for a possible stint in the first sergeant career field.

The USAF FSA offers a one-week training course for those interested in volunteering to act as an Undershirt. Called the First Sergeant Symposium, the course is designed for the non-diamond-wearing volunteer. Instructors from the USAF FSA travel throughout the year to hold these symposiums, offering training in the most important, selected topics necessary for an Undershirt to handle the major first sergeant duties in the absence of your formal diamond-wearing first sergeant. SMSgt Phil Topper is the director of operations for the USAF First Sergeant Academy and adds a great point, saying, "The First Sergeant Symposium is not targeted just at SNCOs. This course is open to anyone interested in helping out the First Sergeant on an interim basis. Section commanders, young officers, and even commanders are welcome to attend—we've had all of the above."[11]

For those in your squadron interested in this program, the squadron commander should have them contact any first sergeant or the wing's command chief master sergeant. As mentioned, this one-week course travels throughout the USAF. You do not need to wait for the symposium to come to your base; you may send your volunteers TDY to the location that best fits their schedule. Of course, this is unit funded.

The next section speaks to the attributes of both a commander and a first sergeant from opposite perspectives. These perspectives have been captured from many former squadron commanders and experienced first sergeants and have been narrowed down to the top five or six key attributes of what a commander should (and should not) expect from his or her first sergeant and what a first sergeant should (and should not) expect from the commander.

What a Commander *Wants* in a First Sergeant. Expect the first sergeant to be the best airman in the unit—your enlisted corps certainly does. Some attributes of an effective first sergeant include the following:

1. A Strong Leader. You want a first sergeant who's motivated—a person who takes charge. He or she should demonstrate confidence not only to you but also to the troops. He or she adjusts his or her leadership style depending on the situation: he or she knows when to chew out and when to console.

2. A Leader by Example. Just as a first sergeant wants a squadron commander to lead by example, you want your Shirt to do the same. A first sergeant who leads by example establishes high standards that are not just enforceable but infectious to everyone in the unit.

3. An Impartial Observer. Rarely will you get honest, negative feedback from your squadron. Create an environment with your first sergeant that encourages him or her to shut the door and say, "Sir, you're wrong on this matter."

4. A Competent Leader. You need a first sergeant who's technically and tactically proficient and a self-starter who gives you the best advice—in other words, a competent leader. You should count your blessings (and not be intimidated or jealous) if your first sergeant is one of your squadron's pivotal leaders.

5. A Good Communicator. A squadron commander needs someone who can speak and write effectively. Good communication also includes listening. The first sergeant must be able to articulate both sides of a problem to you. He or she can't do it without first hearing both sides of the situation.

6. A Dedicated Leader. A squadron commander wants a first sergeant who cares for the airmen 24 hours a day. The job mandates total dedication—nothing less.

7. A Loyal Supporter. Loyalty is a two-way street. A single breach of loyalty can destroy a good relationship. You have the right to expect fierce and dedicated loyalty from your first sergeant, because that loyalty is fundamental and foremost to you as a squadron commander—not to you as an individual. Loyalty to you as an individual will take time and may come later in the relationship.

What a Commander *Doesn't* Want in a First Sergeant. You may know what you don't want in a first sergeant. You've been in a squadron for a long time, and you probably have been in several leadership positions. You've undoubtedly formed ideas of what you *don't* want in a first sergeant:

1. A First Sergeant Who Doesn't Listen. Some first sergeants have their own agendas and suffer from the dreaded tunnel-vision disease. Your Shirt may not be receptive to new ideas, but you're the decision maker. Be direct, honest, and confident. Help your first sergeant understand that he or she must listen to you as well as advise you.

2. A First Sergeant Who Doesn't Keep the Commander Informed. Yes, you'll both be busy, but you're never too busy to let each other know what's going on. Your division of the workload demands daily and frequent communication. Insist on it. Schedule it.

3. A First Sergeant Who Doesn't Support the Commander. Such statements as, "The commander said . . . . I tried to talk him out of it, but he said . . .," don't promote unity or teamwork. A commander and first sergeant must support each other. When they don't work together, one of them must leave. The first sergeant should feel free to

disagree and voice his or her opinion at the outset; but once the commander makes the final decision, both individuals must be in accord. (The same is true of your relationship with the group commander. Don't return from the group meeting and say, "He said we'll do it this way." The correct response is, "Here's the new procedure we're following—period!").

4. A First Sergeant Who Doesn't Lead by Example. How can you give an airman extra physical training (PT) to pass the PT test if no one has ever seen your first sergeant take it? How can you expect an airman to shine his boots if your first sergeant's boots always need a shine, and the uniform looks like he or she slept in it? Get rid of double standards.

5. A First Sergeant Who's a Desk Rider. Most good first sergeants delegate appropriately, so they spend little time behind the desk—they don't want to be deskbound. If you have a desk jockey, assign projects that can't be done at a desk. If the problem continues, talk it out. One heart to heart is all it should take.

What a First Sergeant *Wants* in a Commander. Meeting the expectations of a first sergeant isn't easy, especially if you haven't had any type of relationship before taking command. But certain qualities will help you. Here's a composite of advice from several first sergeants and instructors from the USAF First Sergeant Academy. These are some of the attributes any good first sergeant wants in a commander:

1. A Confident Leader. The first sergeant doesn't need a fainthearted weakling at the helm. He or she wants a commander who exudes confidence in action, in bearing, and in thinking—one who leaves no doubt who's in charge. Remember, you must be a doer; get out from behind your desk, and check training, maintenance, administration, and your troops. It's better to be a decisive hard-charger who makes an occasional mistake than an indecisive leader who doesn't.

2. An Officer Who Leads by Example. This is not the first time you've heard this saying, right? Lead by example in everything you do—everything!

3. A Leader Who Cares for the Airmen. Your first sergeant wants a commander who respects, loves, and protects every airman in the squadron. This quality seems to develop (or fail to develop) early in life. You can't fake it.

4. A Cool-Headed Leader. Don't show your hind end. Be mature and deal with difficult problems in a determined manner. Those who yell and scream are ineffective. A first sergeant wants a patient commander who employs common sense and uses practical application. Agree with your first sergeant to tackle the early signs and warnings that if attacked now, will prevent major problems down the road. Agree with your first sergeant to tackle your most difficult problems first. Sometimes, just your determination to want the hard problems solved first breeds confidence. For some reason, confident leaders have a way of getting lucky.

5. A Leader Who Trusts the Noncommissioned Officers. Words do not accomplish this feat of trusting your noncommissioned officers (NCO)—actions do. Show trust for your NCOs by giving mission-type orders to demonstrate their ability. Make your goals, vision, and standards clear, then let your NCOs perform. Listen carefully to your senior enlisted personnel. They, more often than not, have been performing the mission of the squadron longer than you have. Show them respect by listening to what they have to say. Don't clobber them the first time they make a mistake.

6. A Leader Who's a Buffer. Be the buffer between the group/wing, staff, and your unit. Filter out any detractors and unimportant community details—but in a positive way: "We'd love to help with that project, but we're two days away from deploying to the field for a month," said one security forces squadron commander. Commented another: "We were the only squadron in the entire wing chosen for the task. When we return, let's get together, review the bidding, and maybe we can help

then." In other words, keep the mission first and protect your people against the peripheral stuff and the "nice ifs."

7. A Leader Who Admits Mistakes. No one's infallible. With the powers you have as a squadron commander, you may begin to think you're incapable of error, but you will make mistakes. Be big enough to admit you're wrong and learn from it. Then don't make the same mistake twice. Admit mistakes to your troops; it will encourage honesty and candor in them, and they'll respect you for showing you're human!

What a First Sergeant *Doesn't* Want in a Commander. A normal, healthy first sergeant "ain't bashful." He or she will quickly tell you what qualities guarantee failure in a squadron commander. These examples relate to all members of your squadron as well:

1. A Commander Who Won't Listen. Your first sergeant wants and needs to be heard. First sergeants may not always be right (but neither are you), but their experience and position warrant your listening. You don't have to agree with every recommendation, but you should listen. Ensure they have unfettered access to you 24 hours a day.

2. A Commander Who's Too Ambitious. This commander accepts every task regardless: "Bring on the world . . . we can handle it" is the credo by which this type of commander lives. Expectations of the unit are unrealistic, and the resulting pressure on the unit causes low morale and inefficiency. Know when to say no!

3. A Commander Who's Indecisive. A commander who can't, or won't, make a decision keeps a unit in the cellar forever. A first sergeant usually can live with a mediocre decision more easily than with no decision at all. When you've considered the alternatives, the options, the "on-the-other-hands"—decide. Don't think out loud in front of your NCOs and unit personnel. What they need from you are the magic words, "Okay, here's what we're going to do." And, then do it.

4. A Commander Who Wings It. The commander who wings it acts first and thinks second. The unit has no direction

and no standards because everything's spur of the moment. If you tend to make decisions that way, force yourself to hold planning sessions. Tell your first sergeant to schedule a planning meeting—say once a month; do nothing else but review your current situation and plan where you want to be by a specific time. Sometimes, a commander won't have time to plan but must decide based on the best available information at the time. As a team, you and your first sergeant can do it!

5. A Commander Who Micromanages. Micromanagement drives any first sergeant up the wall, and it's especially tough on good first sergeants. A micromanaging commander doesn't know how to give a mission-type order. He sends an unfortunate signal to his subordinates: "I don't have confidence in you." Delegate and give mission-type orders. Your subordinates won't grow if you don't.

6. A Commander Who's a Desk Rider. A commander who is most comfortable at a desk never will survive. Paperwork and correspondence are important but not at the expense of your unit's personnel. You can't know the pulse of your squadron if you never leave your desk. Visit most often the areas of your squadron you feel least comfortable with.

Tell your first sergeant to feel free to remove you from your chair if necessary. And, promise to return the favor: This desk-riding disease is contagious; first sergeants also can contract it. My first sergeant would bust in my office occasionally and say, "Let's go walk the line, sir." And, we did. Remember, routine paperwork usually can be done more quickly and efficiently early or late in the day, with fewer interruptions.

Depending on the size of your unit, you may not be authorized a first sergeant. As such, you'll likely share a Shirt with one or more squadrons in your group. These group-level first sergeants are equally effective, but you may not enjoy the same commander-first sergeant relationship as you would if one were assigned solely to you. "Do not worry," mentioned Lt Col David Hudson, "This turned out not to be a big deal. Because I didn't have that many folks assigned to my squadron, and the fact that the average age of the personnel was older than most, I fortunately didn't have very many discipline problems. I was also able to control morale issues as well. When I did need the services of a First Sergeant, getting attention from the air base squadron Shirt was not difficult at all."[12]

Counseling

Counseling those in your command will be a given. Counseling, in this context, is distinctly different from formal feedback (see "Feedback Sessions," chapter 4). You will surely spend a great deal of time counseling those in your unit. Like many other things, this can be good counseling or bad counseling. As a minimum, you'll be responsible for counseling your immediate subordinates. But, as the commander, you must be prepared to counsel everyone under your charge as necessary. Note: Don't let your flight commanders and senior supervisors off the hook. They have an important role in counseling, too, and should be equally responsible. One of the first questions I asked when my unit's personnel came to me for counseling was whether or not they had spoken to their supervisor. And, be prepared to handle the situation when they come to you for counseling *about* their supervisor.

One common thread of advice came from nearly every squadron commander interviewed when the subject of counseling arose: be honest and forthright. Said Colonel Hunt, "It is extremely important to be brutally honest when offering counsel and advice. I didn't know how to candy-coat bad news, so I started being very candid. If someone came to me to ask me where they stood in the squadron pecking order, I told them fairly and honestly. It would have served absolutely no purpose to let them believe they were doing better or worse than they actually were. It would give them a false sense of security and wouldn't give them the tools and direction to perform better."[13]

Other types of commander-initiated counseling sessions aren't entirely pleasant. Often you may have to counsel a squadron member about a discipline problem, poor progression of duty-related performance, or because of off-duty actions not consistent with good order and behavior. This type of counseling requires special preparation from the commander

---

Proverb for Command

A commander who sets a standard of "zero defects, no mistakes" is also saying "Don't take any chances. Don't try anything you can't already do perfectly, and for heaven's sake, don't try anything new." That organization will not improve; in fact, its ability to perform the mission will deteriorate rapidly. Effective leadership requires leaders who are imaginative, flexible, and daring. Improving the USAF for future missions requires leaders who are thoughtful and reflective. These qualities are incompatible with a "zero defects" attitude.[14]

---

to ensure his thoughts are clear and concise. Nothing could be worse than fumbling around the issue. This kind of feedback must be addressed up front and directly. And, equally important, don't forget to document the session.

I have yet to find the person, however exalted his or her station, who did not do better work and put forth greater effort under a spirit of approval than a spirit of criticism.

—Abraham Lincoln

Recognition Programs

The sky's the limit in what recognition programs your squadron develops and how you choose to support them. You may wish to create a few new ones or divest yourself of a few old ones.

The Air Force already has in place a number of official recognition programs, such as Airman of the Quarter and Company Grade Officer of the Year. Because they occur on a set schedule (monthly, quarterly, and annually), it should be easy for you and your staff to prepare the appropriate nomination packages for consideration in and above your squadron. Make sure you nominate someone for each possible category, regardless of whether you think the nominee has a chance at winning. The winner is often the only person submitted. Place the burden of package-writing on the shoulders of the individual's supervisor, leaving only minor editing for you. Delegating this responsibility helps the supervisor sharpen his or her writing skills and makes better use of your time. "I emphasized to each of my supervisors the significance of such recognition programs, particularly those focused on the enlisted corps and lower civilian grades. Writing AF Forms 1206 [awards and decorations nomination packages] is, in any person's book, a pain; so there needs to be solid justification for that pain—and there is," remarked Lt Col Terry Kono. "You quickly realize that the end justifies the work when your troop wins."[15]

Outside the official USAF recognition programs lies a plethora of other internal options. Most often, these recognition programs are more personal to the unique character of your squadron, and, as such, can be as varied as your imagination allows. Without being carried away by having too many different awards programs, the advice you receive from your squadron's leadership will help find the right balance.

A great forum for recognizing the exceptional actions of your unit (as well as the members within) is through the wing's public affairs office. The base newspaper is always looking for human-interest articles. If someone has done something extraordinary, why not capture it on the front page of the base newspaper? It provides a tremendous amount of visibility not only for the individual but for the squadron as well. Aggressively pursue this idea—it's a good one.

Recognizing individuals (or sections) in your squadron is always a good thing and is something you can't do too often. Said Colonel Black, "I can't pay them any more money, or instantly promote them. But I can say 'thank you' over and over. A pat on the back goes a long way."[16]

Personnel Decisions

An entire chapter could be written on how best to work assignments for your personnel. Many variables enter the assignment process equation but too many for a book of this scope. There are significant differences between officer and enlisted assignments. You have more control over the former. Your group commander, Air Force Personnel Center's (AFPC) assignment action officers, and the MAJCOM functional managers/personnel directorate will all have input in officer assignments.

Assignments

Additionally, you need to emphasize that your personnel maintain a current preference worksheet in the assignment system. As commander, you are a critical link in the process, reviewing officer's worksheets, including your comments, and enabling the transmittal to the MAJCOM. Your SNCOs and supervisors, in conjunction with the appropriate MAJCOM functional manager, will play a large part in controlling the moves for those enlisted personnel assigned to your squadron. Listen carefully to their counsel.

As the commander, you'll find it's critically important to understand the assignment management system and supplement your MAJCOM with self-study in this command course. Get to know how the enlisted EQUAL Plus (Enlisted Quarterly Assignment Listing) works. EQUAL advertises upcoming assignment requirements by AFSC and rank. Members are instructed to review, prioritize, and list specifically their assignment preferences based on the EQUAL list. The enlisted assignment system differs from the officer assignment system, and, as such, is something you may need to study to understand. Your chief, superintendent, or first sergeant can be a big help in this area. Get to know key functional managers at AFPC and at command levels. This is how the commander, working with his or her leadership, can make inputs on where to send personnel (and how to hire desired personnel).

Commanders place a premium on taking care of their people's careers. To best accomplish this, a commander needs to know two things—the individual's record and the individual's desires. These two items, coupled with performance, should enable a commander to guide and counsel people effectively and honestly. Getting a good handle on an individual's record and current performance usually can be accomplished in the first three months of command. Getting to know everyone's goals normally will take longer.

With the advent of AFPC's internet capability, the commander now has personnel information readily available at his/her fingertips. Ordering a personnel brief on a member of your squadron is easier than ever. Create a binder wherein you keep a record of each of your unit's personnel, including a handmade file of pertinent personnel and career information where you can get to it in a hurry. Ensure your flight commanders and senior supervisors do the same. Great idea.

Lt Col Bobby Knight commanded Detachment 1, 605th Test Squadron (Airborne Warning and Control System), Boeing Field, Seattle, Washington. He went the extra step by hanging a large magnetic white board in his office where he kept key personnel information. On this board was a basic wiring diagram of the unit with the name of each squadron member filled in. On the commander's board were added color-coded symbols indicating each person's date of rank, educational level, and PME situation—for example, Airmen Leadership School, Noncommissioned Officer Academy (NCOA), Air and Space Basic Course, Squadron Officer School (SOS), Intermediate Service School, and so on. (Levels of enlisted professional upgrade status also could be applied, including whether the individual had completed 3-, 5-, or 7-level competency upgrades, for example. He remarked that this not only gave him instant visual information, but everyone who came to his office knew that he cared enough to keep personal tabs on his people. Once the squadron personnel saw that the commander was actively interested in their careers and performance, they took an added interest themselves. The boards were not there to promote competition among squadron members but rather to give a commander a better view of each individual and the squadron as a whole.

Civilian Employees

If you are new to civilian employee relations, you must get some training from the experts at your local civilian personnel office. They'll instruct you on the many issues involved with civilian employment, including promotions, performance appraisals, formal feedback requirements, evaluations, and discipline. "Dealing with civilians is a different world, and as the commander it's incumbent on you to understand their system and culture,"[17] said Lt Col Donald Flowers.

If you have a large civilian work force in your squadron (such as found in many civil engineering, transportation, services, or supply squadrons), you will likely have a civilian as your deputy commander. He or she undoubtedly will bring a great deal of experience to your squadron and has probably spent several years at the same location. As you will agree, the deputy commander can be a tremendous help to the squadron commander. Lt Col Jon Roop commanded the 437th Civil Engineering Squadron, Charleston AFB, South Carolina. He said, "There is no greater relationship than the one between a military commander and civilian deputy. The difficulty begins by the fact that that the civilian deputy will normally be senior in age, have more years of experience in the functional area, and have a greater knowledge of the civilian personnel system."[18] The deputy will share at least as much passion for accomplishing the mission, but the deputy does not share the responsibility of command. In the support functional area, the civilian deputy normally brings a greater depth and breadth of the business to the squadron while the commander brings the intangible perceptions of base or MAJCOM leadership.

"How you share the responsibilities between the civilian deputy and the commander is entirely personal and up to you,"[19] remarked Lt Col Wilfred Cassidy, who commanded the 42d Civil Engineering Squadron, Maxwell AFB, Alabama. "All civilian affairs must be coordinated with the deputy—he's (she's) the primary spokesman for the civilian workforce, but they understand that the commander is the sole spokesman for the squadron. They have valuable planted roots in the business and in the community and can be a valuable source of information. I used them as much as possible," he continued.

One thing of which many military members are guilty, for a variety of reasons, is a lack of proper documentation in the civilian discipline area. Like the common real estate phrase of "location, location, location," so it is with the Air Force, except it should be "document, document, document," particularly when dealing with civilian personnel.

Colonel Flowers had his share of disciplinary problems. But, since his squadron included many more civilians than it did military members, the discipline issues he faced as commander often involved a civilian in his command. "Government employees have a completely different system of dealing with discipline than what we have with the UCMJ for active duty personnel. The fact that their actions represent the Air Force, the perceptions of the local community are important. Civilians have labor union representation, and as such, there's a lot more 'red tape' to deal with." He added, "All discipline actions must be worked through the wing Civilian Personnel Office. It usually starts with a verbal counseling, then escalates through written counseling, letters of reprimand, suspension from duty (with or without pay), and, if necessary, termination."[20]

Ceremonies

As the commander, you certainly have a stake in the opportunities for promotion for those in your command. You have a significant role in that process through officer and enlisted performance reports you submit periodically (see chapter 4, "Officer/Enlisted Performance Reports"). But, what do you do when you're notified that one or more of your unit's personnel has been selected for promotion? Again, several former commanders offered some good advice.

Promotions

"I made promotion ceremonies a big deal," remarked Colonel Kono. "It is terribly important to recognize those promoted for their accomplishments, and we thought it was the right thing to do to make it big. After all, it *was* big,"[21] he added. Even the automatic promotions deserve recognition. Every stripe an airman has tacked on represents a career milestone. Senior enlisted personnel respect the progress; the junior enlisted should aspire to it.

Being asked to officiate a promotion ceremony, officer and enlisted alike, is an honor. You've undoubtedly been in the audience of many promotion ceremonies in your career and think this section need not be written. But, as many former commanders will tell you, "It's a whole different ball game when you're the one *running* the ceremony!"

How are you notified of pending promotions? The answer differs slightly when discussing officer versus enlisted promotion notifications. In both cases, your wing's Military Personnel Flight (MPF) likely will have the list of promotees in the MPF a week or even earlier than the announced formal release date. This is done so they can break out the list by squadron, confirm its authenticity, and notify the wing/group commanders in advance to write letters of congratulations. Depending on the techniques of your particular wing, squadron commanders usually are not notified more than two days in advance to allow them the same congratulatory note-writing privilege.

The methods of notifying those selected for promotion vary as much as the imagination allows. Demographics of your squadron, and location of the promotee (TDY), will come into play. It was the modus operandi in my squadron to make enlisted promotion announcements en masse on the formal release date due to the sheer size of the list. It wasn't unusual to have 40 or more E-4s selected at one time. This particular situation did not allow for a more personal notification by me—something I would have cherished—although I followed up each group announcement with a personal visit and note of congratulations (and sent a letter home to their parents).

Some commanders interviewed went to great lengths to make the announcement as special a moment as possible. Some called the selectees the night before the official announcement; some took a small gift and their spouses with them to the promotees' residences; and others surprised the individual in their work space. Lt Col Scott Hanson had an interesting method when notifying his personnel of promotions when he commanded the 99th Airlift Squadron (Special Air Mission), Andrews AFB, Maryland. He often would find his busy personnel flying as flight attendants or crew members for the nation's senior-most government officials. "I'd track them down wherever they were," he said. "We had a method of flight following, and I knew the telephone numbers to contact them airborne. It was neat to be in my office at Andrews, and be able to call them at 35,000 feet over the Far East to congratulate them. It made the announcement much more special."[22] Other commanders, as a method of playful torment, would wait until the afternoon of the promotion release date to make their folks sweat to tease them. To each his or her own.

One common piece of advice amongst the squadron commanders who were asked to promote or reenlist their troops was this: *memorize* the oath! Memorizing the oath does a number of things for you. It adds a definite sense of professionalism to the ceremony; it makes the officer or enlistee feel that you thought enough to memorize the oath (particularly as a commander); and it makes the fumbling with the written oath go away. Memorizing the oath is easy. The officer promotion oath of office reads:

> I, (state your name), having been appointed a (grade in which appointed), United States Air Force, do solemnly swear (or affirm) that I will support and defend the Constitution of the United States against all enemies, foreign and domestic; that I will bear true faith and allegiance to the same; that I take this obligation freely, without any mental reservation or purpose of evasion; and that I will well and faithfully discharge the duties of the office upon which I am about to enter, so help me God.

While the oath of office isn't a mandatory part of the USAF promotion ceremony, it bears enormous weight to the promotee in terms of ongoing commitment to duty. It also reminds the audience of our enormous responsibilities. I encouraged it at every opportunity.

Nonselectees

This section would be incomplete if it didn't address the unpleasant situation of having to notify those of your personnel *not* selected for promotion. A list of nonselectees will also be compiled by the MPF, and how you handle the delicate situation is entirely up to you as the commander. In many officer cases, particularly field-grade officer nonselects, the wing or group commander will handle this task for you. In most other cases, this task becomes your responsibility.

One of the best insights I heard while conducting this subject of research came from Lt Col Dave Bujold, who commanded the 413th Flight Test Squadron, Edwards AFB, California. He faced the situation of notifying those not selected for promotion more than once. "I started the process early when discussing the individual's PRF (Promotion Recommendation Form). If I thought their record was mediocre, and he or she hadn't completed an advanced academic degree or the appropriate PME, I let them know that their chances for promotion were at risk—and to prepare for that fact, now."[23] He went on to say, "I was polite and sensitive to the matter, but I was also very forthright. I told them that everyone gets passed over sooner or later, unless you're the Chairman [of the Joint Chiefs of Staff] (CJCS). It just happens to some earlier than others."[24]

When the inevitable day arrived, Colonel Bujold handled the matter with tact and sensitivity. "I went to personally speak with the individual the evening before the official release date. The goal is to make sure the guy/gal isn't ostracized more than the news itself already makes him/her. Put your arm around them and remember this is a big deal. Ignoring the situation only makes it worse,"[25] he added. Great advice.

The main difference between enlisted and officer nonselections is that the enlisted promotion system is not a one-time deal. Officers meet a one-time, on-time promotion board, where, if not selected, they may compete for the highly competitive Above the Promotion Zone board. The enlisted promotion system works on an order of merit. They academically test for a series of points and also receive points for time in grade and decorations. If they amass enough points, they are selected for promotion to the next grade. If not, they compete again the following year until they run into a high-year tenure wall and have to separate or retire. This situation offers a different opportunity for the commander to counsel their enlisted personnel. Several days after the official promotion release date, you, as the commander, will receive the breakdown of points for each of the nonselectees. It is your responsibility to pass the information on to them. This may also be a good time for selective feedback sessions. Sharing the individual's promotion scores with them not only shows that you care about their professional career and potential for advancement, it has a more practical aspect: it identifies the specific weak areas in need of further study and attention.

Officer or enlisted, promotions are significant career milestones; human nurture inevitably ties self-esteem to the promotion process. Lt Col Lori Montgomery commanded the 49th Medical Operations Squadron, Holloman AFB, New Mexico. She said, "I had an officer not selected for promotion. This was the officer's second time nonselect. She was somewhat expecting this, but it didn't make it any easier. You need to look them straight in the eye. I made sure they know they are still valuable to the squadron and the Air Force, and I gave the member the option of taking the next day off to collect his or her thoughts. I arranged for her schedule to be covered, and I called to see how she was doing. You also need to ensure someone is there to take care of them. My door was always open to discuss any future career options. You need to make sure you have some type of support system."[26]

Reenlistments

Being asked to reenlist one of your unit's enlisted personnel will be another highlight of your tenure in command. The person who is up for reenlistment has the choice to have any commissioned officer read them the oath, so if they choose to give you the honor, take it with pride. This happens only once every several years in their professional careers, so take the event seriously. Although the event is a short one, lasting only a few minutes, all former squadron commanders advised to make it as big a deal as you can (and as the enlistee wishes). The enlistment oath reads:

I, (state your name), do solemnly swear (or affirm), that I will support and defend the Constitution of the United States against all enemies, foreign and domestic; that I will bear true faith and allegiance to the same; and that I will obey the orders of the President of the United States and the orders of the officers appointed over me, according to regulations and the Uniform Code of Military Justice. So help me God.

It pays to practice the oath several times in front of a mirror or family member, because it's easy to forget the exact wording when you're standing in front of dozens of people. Also, it will be helpful to both you and the enlistee if you have pre-planned breaks in the oath where you must stop for them to repeat your words. Practicing to memorize this takes a little time, but it's worth it.

Retirements

"I made a huge deal out of retirement ceremonies," said Colonel Black. "For someone to have given 20 or more years of their lives faithfully and honorably in support of their nation, I thought it was extremely important to take the necessary time to have a special ceremony, not just for the retiring individual, but for their families as well."[27]

It may be understood, but when things get busy, it's easy not to take the time to do a dry run of the ceremony. This is a mistake. Usually done the day before the event (to allow for extra time to make corrections as necessary), the minimal efforts from a focused 10-minute practice will pay huge dividends the next day. Ask some relevant questions: Where will the flags be placed (United States and squadron guidon)? Have you requested a photographer? Will music be played, and if so, who's responsible for the communication equipment? Who will proffer the retirement decoration? Has the narrator reviewed the script for accuracy and completeness? Who has been invited—family, friends, and distinguished visitors? These are just a few important questions to ask. If it helps, develop a checklist to follow every time.

Rehearse the sequence of events—something you can readily get from the wing protocol office. Ensuring you know where the official retirement orders are read and when unit gifts will be bestowed not only makes it right but also ensures a smooth and polished ceremony. This is a once-in-a-lifetime event for the retiree and his family, so make it special.

When a member of your unit asks you to be the officiating officer, take the moment to ask some key questions. The obvious would include the individual's desire for the date, time, and place of the ceremony. Will it be held in a squadron room, or will you have to make arrangements elsewhere due to the size of the group? For example, while I was assigned to Ellsworth AFB in Rapid City, South Dakota, I was privileged to officiate several retirement ceremonies at the Mount Rushmore National Monument (which required advance reservations and special transportation). Who will attend? Mom, dad, aunt, uncle, small children, minister, or close neighbor? Are any of them elderly or handicapped requiring special assistance? Are there any very important people on the list, like a retired general officer or current wing commander? Inquire of the retiring member what, if any, special requests he or she might have that you'll need to fold into the itinerary. Will they be presenting flowers to a spouse or children or any other gift of some type?

In preparation for the remarks you'll be making, don't forget the old saying, "know your audience." Using his or her personal guest list, be sure to recognize those family members and close friends attending the ceremony. Welcoming them to your squadron and mentioning their names at the outset will make them feel more comfortable, as well as serving to let the audience know who they are.

Unless you have a special relationship with the retiring individual where you can shoot from the hip, it is suggested that you pull the individual's service records and read each enlisted performance report (EPR) or officer performance report (OPR), decorations, and awards from which you can build your remarks. Some commanders chose to start their speech with a short biography of the person retiring, highlighting those areas where he or she performed particularly well. Other commanders let the narrator include the member's service history in the opening remarks to alleviate the need for the commander to hog the stage more than necessary.

It is actually quite easy to forget that this is his or her day and not yours. Keep your remarks short and always let the retiree have the last say. Remember that your audience came to see the retiree along with his or her family and friends; they did not come to see the coworkers in attendance. Keep focused on the fact that the entire ceremony likely will be over in fewer than 30 minutes, so be organized. I found that keeping my speech to the bare minimum (no more than five to seven minutes) always let me memorize my remarks without having to fumble through note cards. It certainly made the impression that I truly cared enough to put in the extra effort, and it was very much appreciated.

A common thread amongst commanders who officiated squadron retirement ceremonies was the theme of patriotism. If you are not too familiar with the person retiring, sticking to a common theme that resonates well with most people is a sure winner. Mention, perhaps, how thankful you are to have been asked to officiate, and how envious you are that he or she has given more years of service to the country than you have. Talk about the fact that the flag is standing freely on your stage because of the retiree's efforts to keep our country free. If warranted, mention that through his or her leadership and mentoring, there are many airmen or officers who are ready to take their place—thanks to the retiree's mentorship.

It's a pretty good idea actually to meet with the retiree and personal guests before the ceremony. This will give you an opportunity to make the ceremony a bit more personal and allow you to take a quiet moment to speak with them (and memorize their names). Colonel Black mentioned, "I always scheduled a private meeting with the retiree and their family for about thirty minutes in my office prior to the ceremony. It helped me get a feel for the emotion of the event, and it allowed them all, especially the individual who was about to retire, to take a much-needed breath before we stepped in front of the crowd. It also gave me an opportunity to put everyone at ease by giving them an idea of the sequence of events so there would be no surprises during the ceremony."[28] Good idea.

A couple of thoughts: Although you may personally be very comfortable with speaking in front of a large crowd, many times that will not be the case for the person retiring. Up until this point in the ceremony, he or she has been sitting in the front row staring at you, and when given the opportunity to speak, may get flustered when turning around to see the entire audience. Be prepared to make a comical quip or the like to break the tension. Personally, having had the honor of officiating more than 30 retirement ceremonies as a commander, I found one thing was sure to happen: Even the toughest SNCO will get emotional during his or her remarks. Plan for it. The individual's immediate family also will likely get emotional, and the tears will start flowing. Have a box of tissues close by.

Departures

Although not an official ceremony, as the commander, you likely will be invited to many (if not all) of the going-away functions for those about to PCS out of your squadron. Enjoy them and be thankful that they cared enough to extend you an invitation. Given the particular organization of your unit, it is most likely that a senior member of the flight or work section will take the responsibility of setting up the event. Allow that person to take charge. You'll have many more things on your plate to take care of regarding normal squadron affairs, and it will give the organizer some responsibility to take care of all the details. The event may be scheduled in conflict with your personal schedule, so you may not always be able to attend. Some events will be held in the evening to allow other spouses and children to attend. Others will be held at lunchtime to make it a bit less expensive and to solve a potential baby sitter problem. Bottom line: if you're invited, make every effort to attend.

In this case, don't assume that you should send your deputy commander or other squadron senior leader if you can't attend. Let the honoree make that call. Many times, you'll be invited out of respect for your position as commander, and the inviter might not want your second in command to attend. No big deal. Send a note of best wishes and press on with your day.

Roles of Spouses and Families

The role of the squadron commander's spouse has changed significantly over the past decade. Many more spouses have professional careers today that they enjoy (and would like to continue to enjoy) and simply don't have the time and energy necessary to manage your squadron's spousal clubs—either officer, enlisted, or combined. That's okay. Not one commander interviewed on this subject said he or she felt any undue pressure from the group or wing commander to have his or her spouse build and maintain a robust spouse's club. The significance of your particular spouse's club will be up to you, your spouse, and the rest of the squadron. Frankly, you may inherit a unit in which for whatever reason, the spouses simply don't want to get together on a weekly or monthly basis. That's okay, too.

Commander's Spouse

Your spouse will play an important, and perhaps obvious, role in the direction your squadron's spouses group takes. Your spouse may have a professional career to handle, or you could be married to another military member whose social time is limited. If your spouse wants to take an active role in the group's success, give him or her the support he or she needs to keep it running. If your spouse does not want to take an active role, and your squadron has an existing club, delegate the responsibility to the next senior spouse or other energetic volunteers who are interested. Encourage elections amongst the spouses and have the president of the spouses club organize it and keep it going.

Your role as the squadron commander, though, will be to offer assistance, guidance, and sometimes direction for the group. Offer to speak at the meetings occasionally. Give tours of your squadron's buildings or give a slide show presentation to the spouses to give them a better idea of what their spouse's duties are, where they work, and what they do. This is a great time to articulate the importance of the role of both the military member and the spouse in keeping the unit strong and our country free.

Squadron Spouse Groups

Having said that, it's still important to have some kind of spousal group for those who do wish to participate. The mission and location of your squadron will have some bearing on whether or not your spouse's group is very active or less active. Active spouse groups are very important to those squadrons that are often deployed or that may be located in an overseas or remote area. The camaraderie is important. Conversely, if your unit is located in or near a major metropolitan area or has no base structure or government housing, you may find that there isn't a want or need for an active spouse's group. Several commanders commented on this issue by advising not to push a spouse's group on a squadron that doesn't have any interest just for the sake of having one. It will only be frustrating to you and will take valuable time away from other higher priority unit issues.

One good idea offered by a former squadron commander is to have a "Red Carpet Day" every so often for the spouses and family members. This is an event where you open your squadron for a few hours to show the families what their spouses do for a living. Most commanders would arrange for snacks and drinks or would turn it into a potluck dinner, for example. This adds to the morale of the squadron members as it leads to their pride in showing off the unit, and it allows the family members to feel that they were part of the squadron and extended Air Force family.

Today's demographics of Air Force squadrons have changed. Many of the spouses are male, and that trend will continue to increase as the Air Force recruits more women. This fact alone will call for some innovation on your part and will dictate the framework of your spouse's group. The first place to start with your endeavor is to find out how your predecessor handled the group, if at all. You may walk into a robust, active group that essentially runs itself. And, you may walk into a group that never could seem to get going the way you'd like it to. Regardless, it would behoove the spouse president to test the waters and find out what the group wants to do.

Lt Col Ike Eichelberger commanded a squadron at Kadena AB, Japan, and because of location and culture, had some unique experiences there. His unit had a challenge of having no formal spouses' group. "Many of our spouses were well educated, had advanced degrees, and separate careers that they enjoyed. We had many different spouses in our unit who had different priorities. It wasn't that they didn't care to participate—it was simply a matter of lack of time or cultural differences."[29]

Because members of his unit often were TDY, Colonel Eichelberger took advantage of a Family Support Outreach program that was first tested in his squadron after Kadena AB was selected as a test bed. His unit spent a great deal of time TDY, and he knew that he needed some way to keep the spouses and families informed of what was happening inside and outside his squadron while he was away. He needed an organization to take care of the families left behind. He implemented an organization that mirrored the United States Navy's Ombudsman Program. Colonel Eichelberger, along with the staff at the Kadena AB Family Support Center, implemented a program called Key Spouse—one that is being used at more and more Air Force bases today. The Key Spouse program is a voluntary one designed to enhance existing family readiness services by providing an informal support system at the squadron level. It takes advantage of a small cadre (two or three volunteers) from the squadron spouses' group. It's essential that these volunteers truly want to be the key link between the commander and the spouses because at times they may be busy. They serve as a critical link between the spouses and families of deployed service members, the commander, the first sergeant, and the community. Your volunteers act as a liaison between you and the squadron spouses, giving pertinent information to spouses of deployed personnel (by way of telephone, E-mail, newsletter, or personal visit). The staff of your wing's Family Support Center will formally train your Key Spouse volunteers. This training centers on what base agencies are available in time of need should a spouse in your squadron need help or direction. The Key Spouse program gives spouses another avenue for assistance in addition to the traditional military chain of command. Whether you choose to have separate Key Spouses from your officer and enlisted personnel will be completely up to you and will likely depend on your squadron's size and officer/enlisted ratios.

Your first sergeant will also play an important role here. He may want to play some part in the organization of the program. Talk with him to get his ideas and thoughts before you make any major changes to the existing club structure. Some first sergeants may feel threatened by a Key Spouse program, but they shouldn't. If some wish to take an active role in the matter, let them. But, as always, keep a close eye on the situation and step in only when necessary. Remember, your Key Spouse volunteers are separate and distinct from your *spouses'* club. Colonel Eichelberger added, "The Key Spouses are not the spouses club party planners. Their role is much more important."[30]

Squadron Family Activities

Most commanders, regardless of the size of their particular units, made every attempt to have some type of family event that involved the entire squadron, whether it was a summer picnic or winter holiday party.

One commander was fortunate to command a squadron with an active spouses' group. The group had multiple parties and family get-togethers throughout the year. "Our base was somewhat geographically isolated, and since it was in a small town, there wasn't [sic] a great deal of spouses who were employed in the community. And, since I knew most members cherished their weekend private time, I asked permission to hold our picnic at a downtown park during the workweek. We shut the squadron down and had a great time with all the families," she said.

Lt Col Michael Prusz added, "Make it fun to be part of the organization. The list is endless for activities I have seen effective leaders accomplish: family functions at a pumpkin patch, family events at a local amusement park, Missouri River cruises, and so on. Don't make it 'mandatory fun,' but instead make it an event that people want to do."[31]

Taking the opportunity to host a children's Easter/spring party or Christmas/holiday party will be well worth your time and efforts. Have the kids assembled and then have the Easter bunny show up in one of your unit's vehicles (or airplane, as one commander arranged). The children will love it, and it will add another dimension to your arsenal of creating and keeping morale high. Delegate as much as you can, and the effort will be dispersed enough so no one gets burned out.

Colonel Black arranged some type of casual squadron social once every three or four months. He said, "We usually tied the event to a particular time of year, whether it was summer burger burn or a fall camp-out. There was no pressure to attend, and those that did had a great time."[32]

In sum, not only do the people in your squadron make or break your unit's mission, without them, you'll *have no* unit mission. As the commander, you're there to lead your people, who will, in turn, accomplish the mission. Do it well, and the rewards will be plenty.

Notes

1. Lt Col Michael Retallick, interviewed by author, Maxwell Air Force Base (AFB), Ala., 7 August 2001.

2. Lt Col Robert Suminsby Jr., interviewed by author, Maxwell AFB, Ala., 3 May 2002.

3. Lt Col Alan Hunt, interviewed by author, Maxwell AFB, Ala., 20 September 2001.

4. Lt Col Matthew Black, interviewed by author, Maxwell AFB, Ala., 15 November 2001 and 14 March 2002.

5. Lt Col Terry Kono, telephone interview with author, Dyess AFB, Tex., 20 December 2001.

6. Lt Col Anthony Rock, interviewed by author, Maxwell AFB, Ala., 14 November 2001.

7. Lt Col Kurt Klausner, interviewed by author, Maxwell AFB, Ala., 31 August 2001.

8. SMSgt Walter Lilley Jr., interviewed by author, Maxwell AFB, Ala., 18 September 2001.

9. Lt Col Dennis Jones, interviewed by author, Maxwell AFB, Ala., 21 November 2001.

10. Ibid.

11. SMSgt Phil Topper, interviewed by author, Maxwell AFB, Ala., 8 February 2002.

12. Lt Col David Hudson, interviewed by author, Maxwell AFB, Ala., 3 December 2001.

13. Hunt interview.

14. Army Field Manual (FM) 22-100, *Army Leadership*, 31 August 1999.

15. Kono interview.

16. Black interview, 15 November 2001.

17. Lt Col Donald Flowers, interviewed by author, Maxwell AFB, Ala., 6 December 2001.

18. Lt Col Jon Roop, interviewed by author, Maxwell AFB, Ala., 22 March 2002.

19. Lt Col Wilfred Cassidy, interviewed by author, Maxwell AFB, Ala., 25 March 2002.

20. Flowers interview.

21. Kono interview.

22. Lt Col Scott Hanson, interviewed by author, Maxwell AFB, Ala., 20 March 2002.

23. Lt Col David Bujold, interviewed by author, Maxwell AFB, Ala., 25 March 2002.

24. Ibid.

25. Ibid.

26. Lt Col Lori Montgomery, interviewed by author, Maxwell AFB, Ala., 24 March 2002.

27. Black interview, 14 March 2002.

28. Ibid., 15 November 2002.

29. Lt Col George Eichelberger, interviewed by author, Maxwell AFB, Ala., 5 September 2001.

30. Ibid.

31. Lt Col Michael Prusz, telephone interview with author, Offutt AFB, Nebr., 27 February 2002.

32. Black interview, 15 November 2001.

Chapter 4

Communicative Leadership

Remember, gentlemen, an order that can be misunderstood will be misunderstood.

—Moltke

There are many keys to effective communication, and as a squadron commander, you must be familiar with all of them. You'll need to communicate with your personnel one on one, in small groups, in large forums, and in front of your entire squadron at times. The method you choose to do so is important because ineffective communication is often worse than no communication at all.

Effective leaders keep their subordinates informed to show trust, relieve stress, and allow subordinates to determine what they need to do to accomplish the mission when circumstances change. By informing your squadron's personnel of a decision—and as much as possible, the reason for it—you show your subordinates they're important members of the team. Accurate, timely information also is a catalyst to relieve unnecessary stress and helps keep rumors under control. This chapter deals with those issues affecting communicative leadership.

Commander's Call

One vehicle for facilitating communication is the commander's call. You've probably attended dozens of them over the past few years, but this may be the first time when you're on the stage and not in the audience. Experienced commanders all agreed that thorough preparation for these events was necessary. A couple of commanders related how they would dry-run their commander's calls completely the day before; many others told me they would have had at least their executive officer or secretary make up detailed note cards for them to review before the event.

105

A commander's call is a more formal meeting for the entire squadron, and its timing usually depends on the commander's desire. Some commanders hold commander's call once a month, some every other month, and some less often. The average was about once every other month. There also may be specific command guidelines for the frequency of commander's calls. Make sure you reference any major command instructions on the subject.

When you hold a squadron senior staff meeting to dispense information, you always run the risk of having the information misinterpreted as it is handed down from mouth to mouth. The forum of a commander's call allows the unit personnel to "hear it from the horse's mouth" and thus runs less chance of misinterpretation. Commander's calls are used for many purposes, such as presenting awards and decorations presentations, sponsoring recognition programs, and providing guest speakers, films, and/or briefings. They also allow the commander to put out much information, guidance, and direction to all unit personnel at once. Many commanders view their periodic commander's calls as their single most important meeting.

"I cannot overemphasize the power of good communication in getting everyone aboard your train, to dispelling myths and rumors, and to getting people to know each other and building a sense of 'us' in that room or meeting area," mentioned Lt Col Roderick Zastrow. "But when you do have a commander's call, keep the awards visible but brief, the topics relevant and short, and the atmosphere appropriate to your leadership needs. Lack of communication will lead to uncertainty, distrust, and confusion. Worse yet, it can lead to lowered morale or safety issues,"[1] he continued.

A word of advice: as a minimum, dry-run any presentation materials or effects well before the event. If you're using some kind of electronic equipment, such as slides, movie clips, or PowerPoint presentations, make sure they've been "flight tested." Does the microphone work? Are the video clips cued to the proper segment? Are the military decorations (and their pins) to be presented physically there? Are the national flag and squadron guidon in place? Has the photographer arrived? A simple checklist will help you ensure your commander's call goes off smoothly. An unprepared presentation by the commander not only looks unprofessional, but it will also be personally embarrassing.

Commander's calls can be full of surprises that will test a leader's calm under fire. One commander related that he was totally blindsided by the unannounced appearance of the wing commander at one of his commander's calls. Fortunately, the squadron commander was slick of tongue—he immediately added the colonel into his current comments and smoothly introduced him to the squadron before the colonel had even made his way to the front of the auditorium. I was surprised myself once by a birthday greeting entering one of my commander's calls—I tried to act calm and cool while everyone got a good laugh.

One commander used an interesting technique with her commander's calls to answer people's questions. Realizing that many young troops are reluctant to stand up and ask the commander a question in a large gathering, she invited everyone to write down any question on the back of his or her attendance slip. She then ensured that each question was answered, either individually, through a staff meeting where the word was passed down to everyone, or at the next commander's call.

Lt Col Kurt Klausner tried a different variation of the standard call at one commander's call. He called his monthly meetings with his squadron "focus groups" because he split up his members by their ranks and essentially held four focus groups in one day—one for junior enlisted, senior enlisted, officers, and civilians. He enjoyed tremendous success because he was able to talk with his personnel in a much smaller group. "Although the message was the same, I couched it differently to fit the audience. Many of the young airmen's vision[s] were just in front of their faces, whereas that was not so with my senior enlisted personnel. Once I established my credibility with the squadron they felt much more free to air any issues with me directly without fear of retribution . . . and express [them] they did!"[2]

You may have the opportunity to command a squadron where your personnel are not all located together, as Colonel

Browne faced as commander of a recruiting squadron. Most of his unit's personnel were dispersed hundreds of miles in every direction from his home office in Little Rock AFB, Arkansas. The efficient use of E-mail satisfied the normal day-to-day communication requirements, but meeting with his personnel called for hundred of hours and miles on the road visiting each of his recruiting detachments. Always willing to accept a challenge, he mitigated the potential problems of communication by holding commander's calls quarterly—on the road.

The number, length, and location of commander's calls were as varied as the number of former commanders interviewed. Almost all differences were related to the size and scope of their squadrons. Most large squadrons, which also were like 24/7 shift-work squadrons, held two or three commander's calls on the same day, whether it was monthly or quarterly. Those officers who commanded geographically dispersed squadrons would hold meetings at the detached location on a quarterly basis and would have all the squadron personnel meet at their home location periodically for a joint squadron meeting only once or twice a year. Some commanders of small squadrons either would hold their call en masse at no specific intervals or not even have a commander's call at all. No regulation requires that you host a commander's call—but command guidance may. It is your responsibility to ensure the squadron's lines of communication are open, and exactly how you choose to do this is entirely up to you.

You may choose this venue to have wing agencies pass out necessary, required annual information. Some used it as an opportunity to clear annual training requirements off the schedule, like suicide awareness, law of armed conflict, or safety. Other commanders elected to use the commander's call forum to award decorations, hand out quarterly awards, and otherwise recognize the successes of their people. Equally different, many commanders chose to hand out decorations in the individual's work center in front of those personnel the recipient knew best. Once again, consult with your senior NCO leadership and deputy to come up with the best forum that fits the particular situation.

News of the Week

I inherited a great program that was already running in my unit. I was faced with the dilemma of having the bulk of my squadron's workforce out on the flight line and away from any current information on a daily basis. Communication by way of bulletin board, E-mail, newsletter, or roll calls wasn't sufficient to keep all informed as necessary. The squadron maintainers would come to work at their assigned time, walk through the squadron to the toolshed to pick up their tools, and head out to work for an eight-hour shift before washing up and going home. It was a constant challenge to keep the lines of communication open, particularly for nearly 500 personnel. My predecessor had a terrific idea. It was called "News of the Week." Every single Friday, I arranged to speak to every single member of the squadron; mid- and day-shift workers gathered at 0700 (for those personnel coming off shift and those going on), swing shift workers at 1500, and all officers at 1530. If I couldn't be there, I ensured my director of operations or senior maintenance officer was briefed. The meetings were kept short, about 15 to 20 minutes, and gave all the "news of the week." It was here where I chose to hand out lower level decorations, attaboys, and general news of interest to the members and their families. It was a huge success. This offered a great opportunity to ensure everyone got the word for a squadron where the vast majority of the unit worked outside the squadron confines, away from E-mail. It broke up the normalcy of a typical commander's call, gave relevant information in a timely manner, and allowed me to connect with my squadron in a more meaningful way. The feedback was exciting.

Squadron Meetings

Among the numerous methods commanders use to get the word out to their people, in-house squadron meetings were the most common.

> *When administration and orders are inconsistent, the men's spirits are low, and the officers exceedingly angry.*
>
> —Sun Tzu

109

Meetings inside the Squadron

The weekly staff meeting is probably the most commonly used method to disperse information in a squadron. It provides the commander the chance to discuss important issues with his or her squadron staff and to provide guidance and direction. However, for the information to reach the lowest level in the unit, the staff and supervisors must clearly and accurately pass on the commander's word to the troops.

You will quickly discover that you need to lead productive meetings. This may go without saying, but you may be surprised to find yourself locked into unproductive, long, and inefficient staff meetings, by your own doing or the doing of others. To mitigate this, have an agenda laid out for the meeting, state what decisions or outcome of the meeting you desire, and then stick to a predetermined timeline. Period. If you or others need to have sidebar discussions afterwards, then tell people to make it happen, but don't hold the entire group for the period. If you need to convene a smaller group for a specific topic, then do so. Don't keep everyone hostage for hours regurgitating old news or noncritical information.

How and when you hold a squadron staff meeting is entirely up to you as the commander. The consensus amongst those who have recently left command was this: ensure you *do* have a staff meeting—certainly weekly, and sometimes daily if the situation warrants. Some commanders had their staff meeting as the last formal function on a Friday afternoon to frame the next week's activities and to help prioritize any taskings. Others held their meetings the first thing Monday morning as a means of starting the week off "on the right foot."

A more common problem you might face reflects today's OPTEMPO/PERSTEMPO issues and the fact that there will be times when no matter how hard your try, everyone you invite will not be able to attend for one reason or another. Scheduling a meeting the first thing early in the morning (before the start of the normal workday) has proven to be the most successful, although not the most popular. The squadron's mission often drives the pace of the day, and if you can capture everyone's attention before the day begins, it allows them to carry your message forward and not be held to the clock, looking forward to a commander's staff meeting later in the day. Effective communication often requires flexibility.

Unit Advisory Council/Airman's Advisory Council Meetings

A proven, effective means of communication within the walls of your squadron involves feedback from your airmen in a group format. Often called a Unit Advisory Council (UAC) or an Airman's Advisory Council (AAC), it is a forum of individuals who volunteer to meet once or twice a month to discuss issues that affect the health, morale, and welfare of a unit. In this meeting, a handful of folks will get together to address any possible wish (or complaint) unit personnel may have. Then, one or more of the council's members makes an appointment with the commander to discuss each item. Establishing and encouraging such a council meeting works to your advantage as much as it does to the airmen who called it. Often, a UAC or AAC will bring squadron-related issues to your attention that otherwise wouldn't come through any other channel.

Generally, an NCO or junior officer (like a section commander, for example) presides over the meeting. It is important to ensure the council is well represented by members across all disciplines of your squadron to give you the most complete feedback possible for your action. As the commander, you should open the meeting with a short remark thanking them for taking the time to represent the airmen's views and bringing these issues to your attention—then leave. Your presence will often stifle the opinions generated within the council meeting, which is precisely something you would want to avoid.

Many interesting ideas may arise from such a venture. Issues you never would have thought of often will come up and may well be within your purview to address and resolve. Items that have come up include such subjects as: "May we use squadron self-help funds to build a unit picnic area?" or "Can we change our shift hours to accommodate the intramural sports programs?" Not all issues raised may warrant your decision, but your attention to them shows that you care. Lt Col Lori Montgomery said, "I found the AAC helpful. They brought

111

up several issues through the Shirt that they thought were important, and gave me another way of connecting with their concerns."[3] As a good commander, you will want to hear each request or grievance. Address each one on its own merit, make a decision, and brief the unit at your next commander's call or appropriate forum.

Meetings outside the Squadron

Squadron commanders spend a good deal of their time each week involved with meetings outside their unit (most commanders will say "too much"). These meetings come in all sizes, shapes, and forms, and their importance to the squadron can vary greatly. Most of the meetings are mandatory—a specific individual or designated representative has to attend, as dictated by some regulation, policy, or higher authority. Most of these meetings are periodic in nature—and hence provide a great deal of advance notice. Other meetings may be called on short notice.

I once had so many outside meetings held one week that I found myself coming and going. How could I be expected to lead my squadron when I was seldom there? Then came an idea: I sat down with my group commander and asked him to review every single meeting that was held every week and tell me which ones he personally wanted me to attend and which ones I could feel free to send a subordinate. This worked great—it freed up some valuable time for me and allowed my director of operations and senior maintenance officer to see what went on around the wing and afforded them a little "face time" in front of the group/wing senior leadership. Regardless, as the squadron commander, you are responsible for ensuring your unit is represented at all of those gatherings. You may pass the authority on to the operations officer, deputy, supervisor, or superintendent, but you can't pass on the responsibility.

One commander from Dyess AFB, Texas, came up with another good idea that she was fortunate enough to sell to the wing commander and wing director of staff. She, too, found herself bouncing around from meeting to meeting five days a week. Her idea was to sell the wing leadership on the idea of having most of the wing's major meetings all on one day and, in this case, on a Wednesday. Instead of having the mandatory wing meetings held at various times Monday through Friday, she asked if Wednesday could be the designated meeting day. The wing commander would have his wing meeting at 0800, followed by the group commander's meeting at 0930. This allowed her and her fellow squadron commanders the opportunity to hold their squadron staff meetings at 1100 or so and would therefore provide the squadron with the latest wing news and taskings. She figured that if she had to attend all these meetings that at least she could plan her week accordingly. The idea caught on (after a little grumbling), and soon everyone was pleased with the predictability she had built.

It's necessary for you to organize a system to ensure your unit stays out of administrative trouble. Setting up such a system can become old and cumbersome, but if one works, stick with it. One flying squadron commander interviewed had a unique system of internal squadron cross-checks to help catch potential mistakes. Whenever the commander received a meeting notice, he immediately gave it to his operations officer, who supervised the unit's ground and flight schedulers. The operations officer then made certain the individual who needed to attend the meeting received a copy of the notice, along with the schedulers. The operations officer also kept a large calendar in his or her office and recorded all upcoming meetings. If the commander needed to attend the meeting, the squadron secretary noted it on the commander's calendar. The commander and operations officer would spend two minutes each Friday reviewing the large calendar for the following week and then crosschecking it with the unit's scheduling boards. Easy to do and pretty fail-safe. The commander related he had few, if any, problems with meeting attendance after establishing this system.

Taking a few minutes at the end of the workweek to plan for the next week will pay big dividends. Be sure to have your deputy, section commander, chief, superintendent, and, most importantly, your secretary attend this meeting. Here is where you likely will catch any errors made during the week that need to be corrected, as well as making sure your key squadron leadership is all on the same sheet of music with you. I can't remember the number of times this short weekly drill saved my bacon.

That takes care of getting to a wing or group meeting, but what do you do when you get there? Simple—you participate, right? Yes, but it helps to be prepared, especially if the meeting is being run by your boss or someone else higher in the chain of command. To be prepared, a smart commander will ensure he knows the agenda before the meeting. This doesn't mean just knowing the topics to be covered but also knowing why the meeting was being held and what is really on your boss's mind. Use whatever means available to gather this information, and these meetings will be easy. Entrusting your secretary to call ahead to the primary person responsible for the meeting to ask what is expected of you will save some embarrassment later. Ask very directly what slides will be shown, and then ask if you can have an electronic copy before the meeting is held. It sure would be nice to know if the wing commander was going to take a look at your squadron's late OPR and EPR rates and was expecting you to speak to the slides. This allows you to come armed with the correct information.

Another point to consider regarding a meeting called by another agency or unit is that it may well be the most important occurrence of their day or even their week. Don't be surprised if those running the meeting believe it to be far more important than you believe it to be. Hopefully, they will understand this fact and will conduct a concise meeting that covers the necessary points but does not needlessly waste people's time. In this same vein, many agencies will want the actual squadron commander to attend. As the commander, you know your schedule and your priorities best, so you should decide who attends based on existing policies and regulations, and what is best for your squadron. Sometimes people outside your unit need to be reminded of your priorities.

One-on-One Meetings

Some of the most effective communication takes place during individual counseling or individual meetings. Many commanders place a premium on their first welcome meeting with a new squadron member and often try to schedule the meeting

114

so that the new member's spouse also can attend. This type of welcome really can put the new member and his family at ease in a new and strange surrounding. Some commanders said they used this welcome meeting to impart squadron or personal philosophy to the new member. This helps everyone get off on the right foot and usually answers many of the questions that result from a PCS move.

Understand that the physical setting for any one-on-one meeting or counseling session involving the squadron commander can influence the effectiveness and outcome of the session. Nonverbal cues in this instance can be daunting. As the commander, you should have total control here. If you want the meeting to be informal, you may want to go to the individual's workplace or meet somewhere outside the squadron.

Meeting in your office, where you and the other person specifically sit, can influence the degree of formality of the meeting. One former Pacific Air Force unit commander had a set of personal guidelines he used for one-on-one meetings in his office:

1. For an informal meeting, the commander and the individual would sit at a table or in two similar chairs.
2. For a slightly more formal meeting, the commander would sit at his desk and the other person would sit somewhere facing the desk.
3. If the meeting called for a strict, formal atmosphere, the other person's chair (optional) was directly in front of the commander's desk.

The same commander also gave me another tip on how to set the tone for a meeting: most of the time a visitor was asked to "come in" or "go in" the commander's office, but on certain occasions the visitor was told to "report in" to the office. These simple phrases, usually spoken by a secretary, first sergeant, or section commander, help the commander set the tone for the meeting.

Another technique a commander can use to facilitate squadron communication is through a "special agent." Often this is the squadron secretary or executive officer whom squadron members quiz concerning the boss's current thinking. They're looking for the gouge. I can remember that many times, if I wanted to get the word out quickly, I'd tell my section commander to put out the word and sure enough, by the next day, everyone had received the word. As good as the above-mentioned communication techniques may be, they all take second place to the commander getting out from behind the desk, walking around the squadron, and talking to his or her people.

A logistics support squadron commander was right on the mark when he said, "It's often better to speak too much to your people than too little. They need to get to know you better." Your people do need to get to know you better, and I believe most former commanders will agree that they needed to work harder at this during their tour of command.

As mentioned before, where (the location) you talk to your people can be just as important. Taking time to go to your troop's workstation can be a big boost to morale. When is also important—on the flight line in the middle of the night in freezing temperatures or at the front gate with your gate guards in 100-degree weather—not only when it's convenient for the commander.

Feedback Sessions

Communication is a two-way street; a commander cannot operate in an information vacuum. All the methods discussed earlier for passing out information can work in reverse. Any type of meeting worth having will involve communication to and from the leader. However, if you really want to know what your troops are doing, seek them out on their turf and listen to what they have to say. "There's a very good reason why you have two ears and one mouth. Try to listen twice as much as you speak," said one insightful commander. Other, larger forums can be effective for getting feedback, but going directly to the individual is the proven best.

Without question, a squadron commander's feedback sessions should never be square fillers—he or she needs to give honest, fair, and complete feedback for a number of reasons. You may be uncomfortable confronting a subordinate who isn't performing to standards. To make it easier for you, you may attempt to gloss over the unpleasant conversation that needs to be held because it makes you feel better. Bad idea. Giving honest feedback isn't about how comfortable or uncomfortable you are; effective feedback is about correcting the performance or developing the character of the individual. It's imperative that you are honest and frank with your subordinates in this situation. If you let people get away with substandard performance because you want them to like you or because you're afraid to make a hard call, you're sacrificing the high standards of the United States Air Force for your personal well-being. You're not developing your squadron's personnel.

First, those who work directly for you are probably the most senior personnel in your squadron, both officer and enlisted. In addition, as such, they more than anyone are key influences to your squadron's successes or failures. A commander who treats feedback sessions lightly is not only unprofessional, but one who robs the individual of an honest appraisal of his or her standing in the organization and the Air Force. This is not the time to be the nice guy.

Second, these sessions are particularly useful tools with which you can guide and mentor your senior supervisors in the direction you want the squadron to proceed. The current Air Force formal feedback system already has a built-in periodic schedule system. There's no stigma associated with anyone being called into your office for other than the intended purpose. This should be an open and candid conversation between the two of you—just the two of you. This is a one-on-one endeavor and not a group session. What is said between the two of you should remain between you both and not be talked about outside your office.

Third, give your personnel the opportunity to give you some feedback as well. Let them know you intend to ask them their opinions before your feedback session to allow them to gather their thoughts accordingly. I believe this is a good idea and one that I used effectively. I was given terrific feedback, both good and bad, that helped to keep me focused on the issues at hand. It's necessary to create an open atmosphere of non-attribution and have a thick skin if you want truly honest feedback in return. Not all commanders interviewed agreed with this philosophy.

Sometimes, no matter how hard you try, people are just reluctant to talk to the boss about certain matters but are perfectly willing to talk at length to their own peers. Here again, a special agent comes in handy—someone who has the ear of everyone, the informal leader, the old head to whom everyone turns for small problems. Your first sergeant may easily fill this role. Many commanders related how they often asked this person to help keep them informed of the unit's health and morale. Commanders shouldn't operate in a secretive or clandestine manner but in an open way, acknowledging that some things just don't naturally float up to the boss.

Another area that tends to fall into anyone's uncomfortable zone is the issue of dispensing honest feedback, whether it's done informally at a sidebar or formally during the midterm performance report review. In either instance, the adage of "honesty is the best policy" applies. Countless times, many commanders agreed that although it may be a bit unpleasant for you at first, the individual spoken to almost always agreed that they'd rather have it straight than for the commander to give them false hopes or expectations. "As the commander, you can't afford to always be the nice guy. I wasn't running a popularity contest," said one recent squadron commander, adding, "My job was to tell the troop exactly where he stood, in no uncertain terms, so he could grow and mature."

Lt Col Michael Prusz agreed and added, "Communicate, communicate, communicate. Successful leaders deliver the news, both good and bad. I've noticed the adverse impact of the leader who delivers the good news and allows the bad news to filter by way of unofficial channels versus the respect gained by the leader who, while not enjoying the moment, delivers the bad news in an open but honest atmosphere."[4]

This commander is right on target. One of the very reasons for the formal feedback requirement for you and the person you rate is to give him or her the honest feedback he or she deserves to make a midcourse correction if necessary before his or her annual OPR/EPR needs to be written. It should be no surprise to anyone when the performance report is written as to how well the individual is performing.

Routine Paperwork

There are many pulls on a squadron commander's time during the day. Most commanders will rate attending to the mass of paperwork piled up in their in box as one of their least favorite activities.

The Need to Prioritize

Commanders would rather spend most of their time with their mission and their people. To help ensure that you, as commander, have more time for those duties you prefer to do, I offer three suggestions:

1. Prioritize your work, by either due date or importance.
2. Develop efficient systems to effectively work those things you may not particularly like to do.
3. Be proactive with your personal schedule.

Through the commander's in box passes most pieces of paperwork, either coming into the unit from external units/agencies or going out of the unit to these same locations. The exact volume of paperwork the commander sees should be up to the commander! Most units have administrative personnel—a secretary, executive officer, or administrative clerk—who screen correspondence going to and from the commander's office. I was fortunate to have an exceptional section commander. Given his maturity and experience, I allowed him to sign almost every piece of paperwork that didn't need my specific signature, and I trusted him to keep me informed of those issues needing my attention. I was never blindsided, and he felt great about being trusted with greater responsibilities.

As a new commander, you may want to see 99 percent of the paperwork. However, as you become more comfortable with the environment, you should decide what items you do not want or need to see, and then direct how this paperwork should be routed in and out of your squadron. All paperwork is of some importance to your unit, but as a couple of commanders emphasized to me, some paperwork is more important than others!

Every commander has his or her own priorities regarding the importance of the many types of paperwork. A vast majority of commanders place performance reports (officer, enlisted, and civilian) on top of their lists. Nomination packages for awards and decorations usually come in second. Quality and timeliness are critical to both performance reports and nomination packages, and errors in either will get the paperwork bounced back for correction. Worse yet, tardiness here can get you in hot water or cause large problems for the ratee or nominee. One commander related how an oversight in his squadron's administration process nearly cost one of his officers a chance at meeting a competitive test pilot application board. Because he failed to realize that an OPR was past due, the officer in question would have met the board without a current OPR on the top of his record—an OPR that could have significantly played to the board's interests (in his favor) because he had recently completed a master's degree and accomplished several important things in a position of greater responsibility. "Thank goodness for FedEx," he added.

How do you best ensure quality and timely packages? Many commanders recommend developing some type of internal system to accomplish and track these tasks. Realizing automated systems are necessary for mass monitoring of report due dates, it is extremely important to understand the potential fallacy of these systems. Junk in, junk out. The individual and supervisor must take the initiative to watch closeout dates and must be proactive about reporting them. This tactic wins easily. Another key for all commanders—don't procrastinate. Just because the inbox is the least favorite task, don't put it off—it will only get worse.

A couple of good examples were related: A squadron commander writing a performance report on one of his flight commanders started the process six to eight weeks before the report had to be out of the unit. He first had a counseling and feedback session with the ratee and then had the individual take a week to supply the commander with any additional information that might be applicable to the report. The commander told the ratee not to attempt to write the report himself.

Once the commander received the ratee's last input, he sat down and personally wrote the report. This particular commander was determined to write performance reports himself. He told me that on countless occasions during his career, he had been told to write his own report, and he wanted to eliminate that kind of action in his unit.

After his secretary typed the first draft, the commander edited his own work and the secretary typed a second draft. This draft then went to the section commander and the secretary for their edits. The commander's policy here was "no pride of authorship"—anything was fair game. His object was to obtain a good, solid critique and edit of an important document. The performance report bounced around the offices of the commander, section commander, and secretary a couple of times until they were satisfied with the product. The commander certainly was the driving force and had the last say, but he felt the involvement of his two trusted workers greatly added to the quality of the final product. The performance report normally left the squadron two or three days early. The commander in this example told me this system worked well for his two years in the saddle. Everyone had a specific job—the section commander kept close track of upcoming reports and closely coordinated actions with the Military Personnel Flight; the secretary kept precise files and computer disks on the reports; and the commander stayed on top of and ahead of his tasks. Teamwork paid off!

Another example occurred as a decoration nomination package was being prepared on a master sergeant who was a branch chief in a large maintenance squadron. The commander in this story told me his first action was to meet with the unit superintendent (a chief master sergeant) and the maintenance supervisor (a major) to decide what decoration was appropriate for the departing individual. This meeting occurred six to eight weeks before the package was due out of the unit. The section commander, as in the previous example, was responsible for tracking all suspenses of nomination packages. In this case, the decision was for a Meritorious Service

Medal, which requires a good deal of paperwork that might require approval off base.

This particular squadron also had an awards and decorations NCO who was responsible initially for writing and working these packages. The commander next would sit down with this noncommissioned officer to explain what type of nomination would be developed, any particulars the commander wanted incorporated in the package, and when the first draft was due to the secretary for typing. The commander also suggested who the awards and decorations NCO should see in the squadron to gather particulars for the nomination justification letter.

"Happy" Correspondence

Happy correspondence includes personal letters of thanks, appreciation, local attaboys, and the like. It can also include letters to parents.

One of the more successful programs in our squadron was a letter-writing campaign I instituted to parents and spouses of those unit members who performed exceptionally well. I thought it was important to keep immediate family members in the loop on the progress of their spouses or children, and I hoped it would continue to bring together the Air Force extended family into a cohesive environment. It did.

I wasn't sure how to tackle such a voluminous task of writing letters for such a large number of personnel, much less being able to keep track of it all. Here's where a terrific secretary helps.

On one Sunday afternoon early in my tenure of command, I sat down and penned about eight separate and specific shell letters to parents and spouses for happy correspondence. This didn't take very long at all. Then I asked my secretary to type each of these shells into her computer. Every time we wanted to send a letter home, all we'd then have to do was to pull off the appropriate shell, personalize it for the individual being recognized (adding a personal anecdote is a plus), and send it out in the mail. I usually would send a letter home for those who were promoted, those who graduated from professional military education (all levels), those who succeeded in professional upgrades (enlisted 3-, 5-, 7-, and 9-levels, aviator instructor up-grades, and the like. It took little time under this organization.

Of the many things we accomplished, writing letters home was the most successful. Why? Because parents and spouses never tire of hearing good things about their family members, and it added yet another dimension to the team concept. You and I might not think a letter from the squadron commander is a big deal, but the average American does. About 50 percent of the time, parents or grandparents would write me thanking me for taking care of their children. Very often one of my squadron's personnel would tell me that their family would actually make copies of the letter to send to extended family members, and more often than once, would frame it for their wall.

Having this plan of attack with your secretary makes a po-tentially nightmarish administrative problem all but go away. One word of caution: save every letter you write as a separate document under the individual's personal file name. This en-sures that you don't forget that you've written the family before for another happy event and prevents you from sending the same shell. If the family thinks it is getting a form letter, the in-tended purpose for the letter writing is certainly diminished.

"Sad" Correspondence

Sad correspondence follows the same ideas articulated in the preceding paragraph, except that the letters you have to write are now for less-than-desirable things. I personally did not choose to take this course of action, but other commanders interviewed did, and did so cautiously.

There may be times when you have built a relationship with the family of one of your unit's personnel. As such, at the re-quest of a family member, it might be appropriate to send a letter home explaining why your troop was showing signs of disciplinary problems, was being released from active duty, or the like. A word of caution: if you choose this tactic, make sure you keep your boss informed, and run the letter through the wing's judge advocate office to keep everyone out of trouble. You may inadvertently reveal information that is sensitive or legally binding.

Officer/Enlisted
Performance Reports

No matter the size of your squadron, or what the particular demographics are, you'll have to write, edit, and/or sign many officer and enlisted performance reports. (You may have to write a number of civilian appraisals for the civilians in your squadron, but for the sake of length, they will not be included in this work—just be sure to do your homework in this area as well.) This task, like many others bequeathed to you as the squadron commander, must be at the top of your many significant responsibilities.

Without question, the OPR/EPR is the most important piece of official documentation in any personnel's Uniform Personnel Record Group. It is the bread and butter of performance, usually covering a one-year period. It affects promotions, assignments, decorations, and PME selections, to name just a few. But you know that already. Understanding this is one of the commander's most fundamental responsibilities. You might think that these reports are always perfectly written, on time, and without error, right? Unfortunately, this is not always the case.

Former squadron commanders have offered a number of ways they handled this sometimes huge administrative task. Your goal should be to have a well-written, fair, honest, on-time report, and to that end, you'll probably need to come up with some type of tracking system to ensure success. Although many think that the primary responsibility of alerting you to a needed report is the unit orderly room, this is not the case. Indeed, they may share responsibility with you, but it is in fact the rater's responsibility.

Many commanders had a unit small enough to have a manual tracking system (like an office white board or personnel binder), and some larger squadrons had a detailed method of delegating responsibility to individual flights and divisions. Either way, all commanders ensured that responsibility was levied, all ensured the subordinates understood the OPR/EPR significance, and all understood the commander's personal attention constantly was on this matter. Keeping your people focused will enhance success significantly. If they know it's important to you, it'll be important to them.

Until you get to be a prolific writer, it sometimes takes a great deal of time to write an effective performance report on any one person, much less several dozen. As such, it's important to have a system that alerts you 90, 60, and 30 days out from the date the report is due to your boss for review. Establishing a formal system within the squadron as a means of checks and balances is advantageous. It not only keeps the individual in your crosscheck, it affords you greater flexibility in time. You'll have the extra time often needed to write and rewrite the report. Tweaking is always necessary.

If you fail to have such a detailed plan, it will come to haunt you eventually. In my case, it was sooner. I learned this lesson the hard way. One of my officers was meeting an Intermediate Service School (ISS) in-residence board, one I was well aware of; I was editing his nomination package accordingly. Where I failed miserably, though, was in not catching the fact that not only was I late writing his last OPR, I completely missed it by two months! The wing commander (and everyone else) was furious with me, as they rightly should have been, and I was fortunate to recover quickly by faxing his completed report directly to the board. Thankfully, he was selected for ISS, but I was disappointed in my lapse of responsibility. I can't overemphasize the importance of the officer and enlisted performance reports, and the need to have a good report *written on time.*

Interestingly enough, the many commanders interviewed for this book viewed the OER/EPR process completely differently. Granted, while the intent of the performance rating system is for the rater to write the report, have the next section written by the additional rater, and then send it off to the endorser, this, too, is not always the case. Lt Col Anthony Rock commanded an F-15C training squadron, which had a large number of junior officers assigned. As such, he had a good number of performance reports to review in any given month. He certainly could have written them all himself, but he also saw the need to mentor his junior officers in the fine art of official writing. "I opted to have the OPR author submit a draft OPR that included my comments as the additional rater. In this way, they could compose hard-hitting impact bullets and practice writing as a commander might. The real benefit to this learning opportunity was realized when I reviewed the product with the author and explained to them why the final product was preferable to their draft. I saw it as part of my responsibility as part of officer professional development." He added, "It was not without tremendous oversight. It took a great deal more of my time to help rewrite the report, with the junior officer present, but I thought it important that he have some practice with me before he started to write them on someone else."[5]

Open Door
(or Screen Door) Policies

"My freedom to gather information of daily occurrences in the unit was significantly different from that during my previous duties. As a new commander, I found that people were less willing to come to me with bad news or problems until I could convince them that when I said 'Open Door,' I really meant it,"[6] said Lt Col Marc Okyen, who commanded the 32d Student Squadron, Maxwell AFB, Alabama. Here are a couple of tips he used to make this policy work:

1. Never shoot the messenger.
2. Never shift the blame when a problem comes to you, even when you have a million things going on.
3. Take time to talk to your people.
4. Concentrate on what they're saying as if they are the most important people in the world.

An open door policy works well if used properly. Once your squadron personnel realize that you are willing to stop work and listen to them, they will begin to frequent your office. You have to be careful here—once you announce an open door policy, you have to follow through and not put off anybody who may come with a problem or information. You could be opening a floodgate that once opened, can't be closed. This will likely make it more difficult for you to finish paperwork or projects, but your people deserve your time. One commander related how he worked it: if his door was physically open, it was "open"; if the door was physically closed, he purposely needed the time and privacy. He closed the door only when necessary.

Not all commanders shared the view of having an open door policy. They were afraid that this would allow anyone to have free reign of the commander's time and would undoubtedly take them away from other more pressing tasks, keeping them chained to their desks—something they didn't want to do.

One such commander established what she called a "screen door" policy. This commander empowered her secretary to act as a gatekeeper in this area. She did so by establishing a set of rules and boundaries for the secretary to use when unit personnel had to see her right away. Common sense played a role here as well. The director of operations, flight commanders, squadron superintendent, first sergeant, and section commander, as established by her, always had immediate access. Said Lt Col Eileen Isola, "I emphasized that it was *very* important to me that I was able to give my folks my undivided attention when they came to me. An 'open door' policy did not usually enable that—too many things would compete for a finite period. The 'screen door' approach ensured the secretary blocked time on my schedule for me to devote full-time attention, and other resources, to them. Folks would always stop by, stick their head in the door to say hello, but the 'screen door' approach helped them pause, take a breath, and see if they could address the issue with someone else other than the commander. It helped them to think and focus—and not just react."[7]

Lt Col Jay Carlson thought the use of nonverbal (body language) cues was sometimes warranted. He said, "When I was really busy and someone came to my door, I'd get up from my desk to meet the individual before they came too far into my office, and ask them directly, 'What can I do for you?' and intentionally not offer them a seat. This allowed me to still keep the interest in them and the importance of their visit, but it also communicated nonverbally that you wanted them to get right to the point and that this wasn't the best time for a social visit." He also offered another option: "If the problem is not time critical, I'd tell them I'd like to discuss the matter in more detail at a later time. Then I'd step out with them to my secretary to schedule an appointment, explaining that I'd like some undisturbed time to devote to the individual."[8] This reassures the troop that you value whatever they have to say and are taking the time to do it in a controlled manner, rather than "on the fly."

Some commanders simply let their secretaries know that if their door was shut, it was shut for a reason. There will be times when you are performing counseling with one of your unit's personnel, conferring privately with your boss, taking a personal telephone call, or simply concentrating on critical work at hand and you don't wish to be interrupted. Conversely, if your door were open, it would act as an invitation to anyone who wished a moment of your time to enter. Either way, it is sound advice for you to come up with some kind of game plan and equally important to announce your policy to the squadron.

E-mail

If there's one thing that is for sure, it's this: you may be able to manage portions of your squadron by way of E-mail, but you certainly can't *lead* them by way of E-mail. One of the many tugs on your official life every day will be the use (or abuse) of electronic mail. Some commanders admitted that before too long in their commands, E-mail consumed their time and resulted in their staying behind their desks more often than they needed to or wanted to. E-mail can be problematic— don't let it be.

Controlling the E-mail Volume

Lt Col Randy Kee commanded the 36th Airlift Squadron (C-130) at Yakota AB, Japan. Shortly after he took command, he noticed that the volume of E-mail coming to his desk was overwhelming. He'd often get more than 100 E-mails a day, some of which required responses that were taking up a great deal of his time. "And more importantly, it was keeping me chained to my desk where I couldn't get out to talk with folks. Something had to be done,"[9] commented Kee.

One technique that worked well was allowing the secretary (or section commander/executive officer, if you have one) to act as a buffer between the incoming E-mail and you. This can be done a number of ways. One is to create an E-mail account that catches all the incoming spam (i.e., Yakota: all) accounts and gives your secretary access to clear them out before they get forwarded to you. This essentially filters out all junk mail, relieving you of the timely task of opening and reading them before you hit the delete button. Another option is to create both an organizational account (e.g., 331SOS/CC) and a personal account (e.g., john.doe@randolph.af.mil) for separating official mail from more personal mail. Your fellow communications squadron commander can help you in this endeavor. Also, educate the members of your squadron on the proper uses of government E-mail. Discourage them from sending out specific pieces of information intended for a small audience to the entire squadron, group, or wing.

Lt Col Alan Hunt offered a piece of advice. "I used E-mail to my advantage in helping me store important information for record-keeping purposes. I simply built a separate folder for those issues that I thought might come up again some day, which worked great. I had a complementary filing system—one in my desk drawer and one on my desktop computer."[10]

A technique for you as the E-mail writer to save some time is to create multiple mailing lists in your personal file so you don't waste time hunting down everyone to send it to. For example, you may wish to have a separate account for just your flight commanders, Top-3, or senior leadership. This may save you precious minutes in what is an otherwise busy day.

"Good" E-mail

Good E-mail should be shared with everyone you deem necessary as soon as possible. A squadron-wide attaboy from you might be appropriate after winning the wing intramural sports event or for an announcement of an upcoming quarterly awards luncheon. It should not be used, however, as a means of congratulating a single shop or individual—this must be reserved for your personal visit to make such an announcement. It's just as important that you don't waste the time of your personnel in reading your E-mails as you've encouraged them not to do to you.

129

"Bad" E-mail

Bad E-mail is that which causes embarrassment or unwanted attention on any particular shop or individual. This is in sharp contrast to good E-mail because it's in poor taste to publicly bludgeon someone as a technique to reiterate your policy on any given subject. Remember the old adage, "Praise in public, critique in private."

Notes

1. Lt Col Roderick Zastrow, interviewed by author, Maxwell Air Force Base (AFB), Ala., 3 May 2002.

2. Lt Col Kurt Klausner, interviewed by author, Maxwell AFB, Ala., 31 August 2001.

3. Lt Col Lori Montgomery, interviewed by author, Maxwell AFB, Ala., 24 March 2002.

4. Lt Col Michael Prusz, telephone interview with author, Offutt AFB, Nebr., 27 February 2002.

5. Lt Col Anthony Rock, interviewed by author, Maxwell AFB, Ala., 14 November 2001.

6. Lt Col Marc Okyen, interviewed by author, Maxwell AFB, Ala., 22 March 2002.

7. Lt Col Eileen Isola, interviewed by author, Maxwell AFB, Ala., 1 March 2002.

8. Lt Col Jay Carlson, interviewed by author, Maxwell AFB, Ala., 27 February 2002.

9. Lt Col Randy Kee, interviewed by author, Maxwell AFB, Ala., 28 August 2001.

10. Lt Col Alan Hunt, interviewed by author, Maxwell AFB, Ala., 20 September 2001.

Chapter 5

The Good, the Bad, and the Ugly

When you are in command, one thing's for sure: if it hasn't happened to you yet, it probably will. Fortunately, most of it is positive in nature. This chapter deals with some of the issues you may face while commanding your squadron. The title appropriately grasps the wide range of those issues and attempts to give you the behind-the-scenes insight necessary to handle them.

The Good

Actively recognizing the accomplishments of your squadron members is the best way a commander can build both individual and unit morale. It is incumbent upon every squadron commander to do so.

Decorations

You undoubtedly will present the vast majority, if not all, of the decorations awarded to the individuals in your unit. It is not only the right of the squadron commander; it is your duty.

Proverb for Command

Good leaders see excellence wherever and whenever it happens. Excellent leaders make certain all subordinates know the important roles they play. Look for everyday examples of your folks performing ordinary tasks under ordinary circumstances. Make sure they know that their contributions, although perhaps small by the larger standard, are important to the success of their squadron and the ultimate freedoms our country enjoys. Make them feel proud.[1]

Air Force decorations, whether they are medals or ribbons, are not only an integral part of formal Air Force recognition for an individual's excellence, they also have a lasting impression on the individual receiving them. Unlike the wall plaque or certificate of appreciation, a decoration remains with the military member even after retirement. Ribbons and medals are placed on the service uniform for as long as it's worn. These decorations remind the individual of the hard work or singular distinction acheived, and, when viewed by others, they are a continual source of positive strokes. As the squadron commander, you'll not only participate in presenting the award, you'll be thoroughly involved in the recommendation process for the award. In addition, unlike a unit certificate of appreciation that you can generate solely within the walls of your unit, a decoration requires some outside paperwork and an Air Force approval process.

Without a doubt, being able to officiate at an awards ceremony is more fun than writing the justification for the award, but like many other things, one doesn't come without the other. Ensuring that your squadron has a vibrant and robust awards and decorations program is essential to ensuring that the right individuals are recognized at the appropriate level, and when that is done well and fairly, will add to your squadron's morale.

People appreciate the recognition they receive for their extraordinary efforts but have little tolerance for decorations garnered for less than above and beyond performance. Integrity is a key factor here. Energize your squadron's Orderly Room to ensure your airmen are recognized with the Air Force Good Conduct medal every three years—if so deserving. "Every quarter I'd have the Orderly Room run a scan of those who had the right amount of time-on-station requirements for a decoration. The senior leadership and I would then sit down to review the individual's records to see if they [sic] warranted such recognition. If so, we started the paperwork, and if not, we let the individual know why,"[2] remarked Lt Col Matthew Black. Carefully scrutinize those requests for decorations that come from within the various shops, flights, or divisions within your unit. Ensuring that you have an objective team of individuals who buffer each decoration request will keep the integrity of the system intact and keep you out of trouble.

How is a decorations ceremony conducted? Where should you do it? Whom should you invite? These are all good questions with many possible answers. When in doubt, check with the wing's protocol office for a standard template. Again, the wishes of the person receiving the decoration, the possible venues available for the ceremony, and the demographics of your unit all come into play.

Ask some questions: Where does the individual want the ceremony held? Does he or she want a formal or an informal ceremony? Inside or outside the unit? It's important for the commander to understand the desires of the individual because it is his or her option (in most cases) on how to handle the event. Although this ceremony may take just 10 minutes out of your busy day, it may be a lifetime event for the awardee, and as such, deserves your full and undivided attention.

Many squadrons hold these ceremonies in conjunction with a large unit gathering, often at the beginning of a commander's call. Several squadron commanders thought it important to have the individual recognized in front of the whole squadron where everyone would be able to hear of his or her accomplishments and get the chance to congratulate the troop on the spot. Often the member receiving the award is new to the squadron, and the award reflects work from his or her last assignment. Commanders told me this situation presents a good opportunity to reinforce the unit's welcome to the individual. Ensure that the recipient's family is invited to attend the ceremony. The more a commander personalizes the event, the better.

More often than not, the individual being recognized would rather have an informal setting than a formal one that takes place in front of the whole unit. Depending on the decoration awarded, let the honoree make the call. The more informal awards (Company Grade Officer/Airman of the Quarter, for example) can certainly be held informally. A higher level decoration, though, may deserve consideration for a more formal setting. I was fortunate to have a squadron member awarded the Distinguished Flying Cross for heroic actions accomplished in combat. Although he wanted me to hand it to him quietly, I persuaded him to have a formal event because of the significance of the decoration and the impact it would have on others in the squadron. In fact, I asked the wing commander to present the award. Conversely, individuals receiving a lower level award might prefer to be recognized in their work sections where they are known best. In addition, he or she may want to have it presented off time so their spouse and children could attend.

Although it may sound simple, a number of commanders related how they wished they had practiced the easy task of pinning decorations the first couple of times. You may have watched former commanders pin dozens of decorations on fellow squadron mates over the years but probably paid little attention to *how* they did so. Simply put, the decoration (medal) is usually clipped to the left breast pocket of the individual receiving the award. Take the short time necessary to look at the individual's pocket to see how the medal will be attached. Many personnel who wear battle dress uniforms will have the pockets sewn closed, which may surprise you the first time when you're looking for a solid piece of uniform flap to which to attach the decoration. Today's service dress uniform poses its own unique challenges. With no breast pocket available, you have two options: either clip the medal to the lowest row of ribbons present (being careful not to damage the existing ribbons) or simply attach it to the left lapel, twisting the metal clip to ensure the decoration hangs freely and longitudinally.

Several commanders told me of interesting places where they've awarded decorations, conducted reenlistments, and the like. For example, a civil engineering squadron commander gave an award atop the wing's water tower; a flying squadron commander awarded a decoration while airborne in one of the unit's airlift aircraft; a maintenance squadron commander presented a decoration while wearing full chemical gear on the flight line during a major wing exercise; and a security forces squadron commander recognized an airman during a two-week stay in the field. Lt Col Lori Montgomery had a neat saying, "Have flag—will travel."[3] Once again, the more memorable you can make the event, the more pride the individual wearing it will carry.

Awards/Attaboys

You can thank your personnel in numerous and varied ways. There are as many ideas on this topic as there were commanders who were interviewed for this book—too many to offer here. This fact indicated that rewarding people for a good job is always a good thing and something on the radarscope of each former commander. You may tire of saying "thank you," but you can be assured those on the receiving end will never tire of hearing it. It's cheap, it's easy, and it's meaningful. However, it may become a bad thing if the commander offers awards and praise when they truly aren't justified, thereby diluting the entire process.

Lt Col Kurt Klausner believes "squadron coins are always welcomed by the troops," and that while "wall plaques are nice," "many of our folks didn't have an office or cubicle to hang them in." Not giving up, he handed out squadron coffee mugs, which became a huge hit "and before too long became *the* thing to have. Our folks loved being seen with and recognized with something different like a coffee mug because they can carry it around as a matter of pride."[4]

Quarterly awards programs are also a viable form of recognizing your airmen, noncommissioned officers, senior noncommissioned officers, civilians, and officers. Your first sergeant is generally the one who is responsible for these enlisted programs, and will likely have a board of senior enlisted members of your squadron to help organize and recognize those exceptional members put forward for consideration by their supervisors. This is a formally announced program and includes an interview process, often in service dress uniform, before this board. Once the winners are announced, they will then compete for the group and wing quarterly awards programs held some days later. Civilian and officer quarterly recognition programs are done much the same way with a different board of evaluators senior in rank to those being considered.

Like any such board, it's critical that you have personal oversight of the process. This will result in the objectivity necessary to ensure you recognize people according to the rules and policies you've set out before the board. Colonel Klausner said, "The airmen know who is and who isn't the hard worker, the blue chip. If they perceive this to be a popularity program, or one where the winner is a fair-haired friend of the chief, your program will lose all credibility, and so, eventually, will you."[5]

Professional Military Education Graduation Attendance

During your tenure of command, you'll have multiple opportunities to attend the graduations of your unit's personnel who have completed a formal education program. By volume, you'll have more Airman Leadership School graduations than any other form of professional military education. These can be great times. "I practically wore out my mess dress uniform," said Colonel Black. "I never missed a single ALS graduation. This is the first formal military education program an airman gets to attend, so this is a really big deal. I loved it,"[6] he continued. Also, because this event is locally held, it permits many other personnel from your squadron to attend.

Most every other USAF wing has its own ALS school on base; therefore, the graduation ceremony will be on base also. This will certainly make it more convenient for you to attend, and it cuts down the time it takes you to rush home to change uniforms!

When attending local graduations, whether it's an ALS graduation or a quarterly Community College of the Air Force graduation ceremony, taking along your spouse adds an additional nice touch. This does several things for you. First, it makes the honoree feel that much better that your spouse cared to attend; and second, it helps your spouse feel like she or he is part of your squadron's team. "My wife felt no obligation from above the chain to attend these events—she just wanted to, and of course I didn't discourage her. She really loved the formal ALS graduations. And she quickly bought into the team,"[7] said Lt Col Anthony Rock. Besides, given your busy schedule of normal weekly activities, this is a time you can be with your spouse outside the home.

Unless you are assigned to one of a very few wings USAF-wide, those in your squadron who are selected to attend NCO and SNCO academies will have to travel TDY. Accordingly, if you attend the graduation ceremony, you'll have to go TDY as well. SMSgt Walter Lilley, an instructor at the Air Force's First Sergeant Academy, offered this advice: "As the commander, it's absolutely imperative that you attend every single graduation ceremony possible. As a minimum, the commander must attend, but if your squadron budget will allow, taking a second person along, like the squadron superintendent, first sergeant, or the individual's section chief is also a great thing to do."[8] I agree. Even though it may be particularly hard on your squadron's tight budget, you should not skimp this one area. PME graduations are attended by almost every commander, and if some reason prevents your attendance, send your deputy. It's that important.

Regardless of which graduation you attend, it's always nice to make it a bit more special for individuals by doing something out of the ordinary. Many commanders would give their graduates a 24-hour pass (to take the next day off) or a squadron coin. Almost all included a personal note of congratulations. Either way, they have spent several weeks out of your squadron and away from their normal duties to attend classes, and they will likely be interested in getting back to their regular jobs. Make it an enjoyable evening for them (and their spouses or guests) and for you.

Birthdays

One thing's for sure: everyone likes to celebrate a birthday. How, and if, you choose to recognize your unit members' birthdays is entirely up to you. A few commanders chose not to do so for a number of reasons. They felt that this was time consuming given the pace and TDY schedule of the unit. But the vast majority of commanders interviewed felt otherwise.

One commander of a large unit had the Orderly Room give him a printout at the end of each calendar month reflecting the birthdays of the squadron's personnel that fell in the following month. Then, on a Sunday afternoon at home, he would write a short birthday note for every individual who had a birthday celebration the next month. This way he was able to write them all at once without taking time away from his on-duty responsibilities. As the particular day neared, he'd either leave the note on the individual's desk or hand it to the person. "This was very well received. Although I didn't know each and every member as well as I'd like to [due to the size of the unit], it made them feel good that I took the time to think of them," said the commander. Once again, a small amount of effort can have a large return on morale.

Others had a different approach. "With today's computer capabilities, the sky's the limit for creativity. Individualizing a birthday card with my personal software was easy and meaningful for the individual. They really liked it,"[9] mentioned Colonel Montgomery. Another commander thought it more personal to call the individual at home after his duty shift. A short five-minute phone call may take less time than writing a note, and it gives an even greater sense of personal attention. It also allows you to review your personnel cheat sheet and to say hello to the spouse (by name) when you call.

One warning resonated from every commander—"What you do for one, you must do for all." Great advice. Once you've set the precedent of recognizing such events, you can't stop, or you'll risk the hurt feelings of other squadron members. There will be times, undoubtedly, when an administrative error will occur, and you don't have the correct dates, but these should be rare. To make sure you don't miss an event due to your TDY or such, instruct your secretary to annotate your weekly and monthly schedules in advance so you can have the cards written or signed for later distribution, even in your absence. In addition, you might want to add your boss's birthday and anniversary dates to your schedule!

New Arrivals (Babies)

This subject, like recognizing birthdays, is left entirely up to your personal wishes. And, like the above advice, if you choose to recognize the new baby of your division chief, you must also do the same for one of your airmen. If you don't, the word will quickly get out that you favor some people over others (whether true or not) and therefore might have a negative impact on morale. This may sound petty, but in the course of human nature, it happens. And, as such, you need to be aware of it.

Your squadron's demographics will play a large part in your decision making here. If you have a small unit, or a unit with a proportionally older crowd that has just a few new arrivals each year, you may want to go all out for the new parents. Some commanders would visit the family in the hospital, bringing a small gift of congratulations. Some would wait a few days after the birth and visit the family at their home. But be aware, this can be expensive for you as the commander.

Check with the leadership of your squadron's spouses' club to see if they have better ideas. In fact, they might want to take this task from you. It would be a good idea because it would not only make your spouses' club feel more relevant with this added responsibility but it would be one less thing for you to do. Make sure you follow this action up with a short note of congratulations.

Those commanders with larger units usually left this recognition up to the individual's work section. They would often pool some money to buy more practical gifts for the new parents, including diapers or clothing. If this is the case, make sure you have your squadron's leadership bring this event to your attention so you can say a word or two of congratulations yourself. Make this a weekly briefed agenda item at your squadron staff meeting. Better yet, make sure you include the good news in your squadron's newsletter, if the unit has one.

The Bad: Learning
How to Use Your Authority

The USAF grants its commanders an extraordinary amount of authority over their subordinates, not the least of which is the authority to administer discipline to those under their command who violate laws or have episodes of misconduct.

Perhaps the best advice is this: Never, ever abuse the authority vested in you as a commander. It may be easy to fall into a false sense of security by thinking you are invincible in command. On the contrary, you are perhaps the most vulnerable to abuse and the one whose authority may be abused. The higher the ladder of responsibility you climb, the easier it is to be caught up in the possible misuse of authority, whether intentional or not. The checks and balances you were subjected to as a junior officer become less evident and seemingly less compelling with advancement—but that's only because to a greater extent, you alone answer for your actions. You may gradually begin to believe that you don't need to seek the counsel of others. You may be at first surprised by, and then pleased by, the freedom of action accorded you as the squadron commander.

Abuse of privilege creates much of the friction between people. The root of the problem is not that privileges exist, but that they are exercised too often by people who are motivated not by duty, but by privilege.

The power you inherit upon taking command is sometimes intoxicating and often overwhelming. Issues involving discipline and punishment have few equals for the commander's attention. Respect for your subordinates plays an important role here. Respect for the individual forms the basis for the rule of law, the very essence of what makes America great.

Proverb for Command

Command is a specific and legal position unique to the military. It's where the buck stops. Like all leaders, commanders are responsible for the success of their organizations, but commanders have special accountability to their superiors, the institution, and the nation. Commanders must think deeply and creatively, for their concerns encompass yesterday's heritage, today's mission, and tomorrow's force. To maintain their balance among all demands on them, they must exemplify the Air Force's core values. The nation, as well as the members of the USAF, holds commanders accountable for accomplishing the mission, keeping the institution sound, and caring for its people.[10]

This value reminds you that people are your most precious resource. As our country becomes more culturally diverse, squadron commanders must be aware that they will deal with people from a wider range of ethnic, racial, and religious backgrounds. It is true that effective leaders are tolerant of differing beliefs as long as they're not illegal or unethical. Being sensitive to other cultures can also aid you in counseling your people more effectively. You show respect when you seek to understand your people's background, see things from their perspective, and appreciate what's important to them. Take every disciplinary action seriously.

Understanding the Difference between a Mistake and a Crime

As a commander, you are quite literally judge and jury over every member of your unit. Take this responsibility seriously. For the first time in your life, you now have the full authority of the law to dock people's military pay, take their stripes, remove them from their on-base houses, force extra duty, or incarcerate them. This is a huge responsibility for a squadron commander and is arguably the most important thing you will do while in command.

Understanding the difference between a mistake and a crime is crucial not only to your success as a squadron commander but, more importantly, to the lives of those whom your decisions will affect. The distinction between a mistake and a crime is not semantic. Rather, the distinction can easily be made that the big difference between the two is *intent* and *knowledge*. Mistakes are generally the result of poor decision making, inexperience, immaturity, and ignorance on the part of the offender. Crimes are mistakes with intent to commit the crime. They are all listed in your *United States Courts Martial Proceedings*, available from your local judge advocate's office.

Let the ruler be slow to punish and swift to reward.

—Ovid

The 24-Hour Rule

One wise general officer offered me a piece of sage advice. He called it the "24-hour" rule. "Never make a decision regarding discipline within 24 hours of your hearing about it—24 hours as a *minimum*," he said. Similar advice had proven successful for every single commander interviewed and had proven a disaster for those who failed to follow it. Very often the first word you hear of an incident is likely wrong, overinflated, or taken out of context. Your first sergeant usually will be the first to be notified, and his experience will help separate the wheat from the chaff before he delivers the information to you.

"When dealing with inevitable discipline issues, it's imperative that you remain emotionally stable. Don't jump to any conclusions. It's important that you're seen as a strong, guiding force. And never, ever jump into a [disciplinary] situation with the first accusation you hear,"[11] advised Lt Col Dennis Jones.

SMSgt Phil Topper has been a first sergeant for 17 different squadron commanders. His experience is vast. He couldn't agree more when advising new commanders to use the 24-hour rule. "For a whole host of reasons, it's important to take the time necessary to clearly think through any decisions regarding discipline. The stakes are too high if you're wrong, and can seriously affect someone's career,"[12] said Senior Master Sergeant Topper.

Rarely does any disciplinary action require immediate attention. The professional security forces members of your wing or the local police or social services departments will probably

---

Proverb for Leadership

Anyone can become angry—that is easy. But to be angry with the right person, to the right degree, at the right time, for the right purpose, and in the right way— that is not easy.[13]

—Aristotle

---

take those that do out of your hands. In addition, it is during this time that you must peel back the layers of the onion to find out what really happened, understand the circumstances in context, and talk to supervisors, senior NCOs, and the first sergeant. Spend time getting valuable advice from your wing judge advocate (JA) office. One of the JA's primary responsibilities is to provide legal advice to the commander. Then, and only then, should you make your decision regarding any type of punishment.

SMSgt Walter Lilley, a five-time first sergeant, offered a typical example of how things on the surface are many times different from what they first appear. "I once had a young man come to my office after bouncing a check. At face value, he made an unlawful financial transaction, but when I dug deeper into the reason for the mistake, he and his wife misunderstood that week who was responsible for depositing the paycheck—and it never was deposited. This was an understandable mistake that the commander and I recognized. We talked to him about financial responsibilities and let him go." He added, "We certainly aren't a one *mistake* Air Force, but we may be a one *crime* Air Force, and this was no crime."[14]

Uniform Code of Military Justice

Unfortunately, the adage of "ten percent of your people take ninety percent of your time" is often true today. Our nation is based on a system of recognized laws, and within the military system, there is a separate and distinct body of laws. The UCMJ provides a single standard for all individuals. It specifies the general nature of offenses against society and special offenses against the good order and discipline of the USAF. With the exception of the more serious offenses, which by their nature also violate the civil code, the UCMJ does not prescribe trial and punishment outright. Military law, in this respect, has more latitude than civilian law with regard to minor offenders. Rarely arbitrary in its workings, it presupposes the use of corrective good judgment at all times. Its major object is not the punishment of the wrongdoer but the protection of the interests of the dutiful.

Administering the system of rewards and punishments falls directly upon the shoulders of the squadron commander. Our USAF way of life requires obedience to a complex system of rules and regulations. Violations cannot be tolerated without prejudice to the discipline of the entire unit. The commander is given considerable latitude in deciding whether to administer punishment administratively within his or her squadron or whether to pursue courts-martial. As always, advice from your wing/base judge advocate general will help guide your decision.

Perhaps the best way of dealing with the unpleasant responsibility of command and discipline of your personnel is to mitigate it at the beginning. How? First is to surround yourself with as many competent NCOs and SNCOs as possible to head off any situation before it becomes a problem. An attentive supervisor likely will see a problem arising well before you or your first sergeant does. This is especially helpful when your squadron is organized so that you have a great deal of leadership oversight.

This is another area where an effective first sergeant can help avert future disciplinary infractions. If your Shirt doesn't already have a working network of information within the squadron, take a proactive role in ensuring he or she (or you) establishes one immediately. Often trouble and difficulties with your squadron's personnel, whether on duty or more often off duty, can be caught before they require formal disciplinary proceedings.

How you handle the physical disposition of any UCMJ action will be left entirely up to you. Your first sergeant will offer some direction in this arena. Before you accomplish your first act of formal discipline, such as presenting an Article 15, walk through the process with your Shirt. Talk about everything: when the troop should report to you, what uniform he or she should be ordered to wear, how he or she should report in, what supervisors will be in attendance, where all the players will stand, whether you as the commander should sit or stand during the presentation, and so on. Each item has different implications.

For example, when I offered an Article 15 to any of my unit's personnel, I ensured they stood before me wearing a service dress uniform, which was something definitely out of the ordinary. My first sergeant advised me to do so not as a punishment to the individual being disciplined but as a walking symbol for everyone who witnessed him or her walking in and out of the command section. Even in a large unit, the word gets around quickly that the standard was high and was not going to be lowered.

A piece of personal advice: Administering discipline was another area that I chose to use as a mentoring tool for my senior officers who were being groomed for command. Many commanders chose this venue for mentoring their senior subordinates as well. Often, many senior company grade and junior field grade officers never have seen a formal nonjudicial punishment proceeding, so I invited them in to see how it's done. With the privacy of the offending individual considered, I'd often have the senior officers stand quietly in the back of my office, outside the view of the troop being disciplined, to capture the experience for when they may be in such a situation. They all remarked how appreciative they were to be invited to witness the event.

There is a sense of protocol during such events that bears discussing. The first sergeant usually will stand to the edge of your desk, positioned between you and the offending individual. "This is for two reasons," said SMSgt Robert Hill, first sergeant of the 37th Bomb Squadron, Ellsworth AFB, South Dakota. "One is to ensure the integrity of the proceedings by signaling this is a formal event, and the other is more practical—I want to be in position to either catch the person if he faints or stop him from coming across the desk at the commander!"[15]

Most commanders interviewed saw the process as somewhat sterile and formal. Rarely would they allow the offender to speak outside his or her legal rights to appeal. Almost all concluded the event with a word or two of advice. "Once the formality of the paperwork was over, I always took a moment to speak to the troop. I told him that what he did from this moment on was totally up to him—he could grumble and complain that the 'system' was wrong, or he could grow up and act responsibly and move on. I made it clear in no uncertain terms that what he did after he walked out my door was completely up to him and would affect him the rest of his life. I encouraged him to take a minute under the old oak tree to decide which path to take,"[16] said Maj Jay Carroll. Good advice.

One subject that deserves brief discussion is how to handle the degree of punishment given for a particular crime or behavioral misconduct. What is the recommended punishment for an individual who is guilty of underage drinking? What is the suggested punishment for someone who fails to show up to work at a specified time? Simply, there is no one punishment for any given infraction. However, there are limitations in place that the commander must consider and stay within when imposing formal punishment. One thing's for sure: You should punish those that deserve punishment. Equal and fairhanded punishment must be based on the individual's record and an understanding of the punishment's purpose. The commander who is afraid to punish anyone by indecision essentially punishes everyone and typifies poor leadership. Equally important is the consideration of, and concern for, punishment for the entire group for offenses committed by two or three specific individuals. Let your judgment guide you as to the proper punishment for the particular crime.

Often I would have two or more unit individuals arrested and charged with the same violation at the same time; yet, it would not be terribly unusual for them to be given different degrees of punishment. For one individual, this may have been the third offense with other unrelated disciplinary infractions in his or her record. However, this might be the first offense for the second otherwise stellar troop. There is no cookie-cutter answer to any question of discipline. Gather your advice from as many sources as appropriate, and you alone make the decision.

You likely will encounter the dreaded late night phone call from the Security Forces desk sergeant or your first sergeant alerting you to trouble with one of your unit's members (or family). This is precisely the time to be calm, listen to what's being said, ask some questions, and then brief your boss as necessary. Lt Col Leonard Coleman echoed a theme consistent through many interviews relating to handling discipline cases as they occur. "The first report, the seemingly obvious answer, is almost always *not* the answer. The second time the answer will usually contain a little bit more truth, and the third is more like reality,"[17] he remembered.

Talking to your boss about issues of discipline is advantageous for both of you. Sit down with your group commander early in your command and directly ask him what he expects of you at 0200 on a Sunday morning when you get the call that a member has been in an incident. Would he or she like to be notified immediately? Would he or she like to know about the situation briefly before reading about it in the morning police blotter? Or, would the group commander rather the call wait until first thing in the morning? Asking these questions up front early in your command likely will avoid some problems further down the road.

The Ugly: Times of Crises

This subject is one that is wide open, simply because what is a crisis to you may not be a crisis to others and vice versa. By crisis I mean those issues relating to deaths, injuries, serious crises, or accidents. Given such a wide disparity of potential problems associated with times of crises, there is an equally infinite number of methods to handling them. Since every possible kind of crisis likely to happen during your tenure of command cannot be addressed here, all advice will be kept general in nature.

The first and most overwhelmingly popular advice when dealing in times of crises is to remain *calm*. When everything (and perhaps everyone) around you is falling to pieces, this is exactly the time that you want to be rock stable—the stalwart for the event. Those around you will feed off your actions, so it's important to look calm in the face of a crisis.

> *Coping with a death in the squadron was far and away the most demanding thing I ever did as a commander. A death in the squadron is usually sudden, unexpected, and frequently under tragic circumstances. It often leaves behind a grieving spouse and young children bewildered by the loss of a parent. It is absolutely the worst experience in the world*

. . . and yet, it is the time when the Air Force community, the larger "family" we treasure, is at its absolute best.

—Lt Col Robert Suminsby Jr.
Commander
492d Fighter Squadron

Death and Serious Injury

This section provides some real-world examples of death and serious injury situations that happened during several squadron commanders' tours and, more importantly for you, what they did about them.

"I had been in command for more than 20 months when I had a young airman attempt suicide two weeks before my out-going change of command. Although I thought I could handle anything by this time, I was not prepared for this near-death experience. He overdosed on an antidepressant and was fortunately saved in time," remarked Lt Col Anthony Rock. "My precommand prep course spoke about deaths and things but only in light of what Air Force programs were available to help in these ugly times (which are many). Nowhere was I taught how to handle the stresses in the affected family or what I should do during the aftermath,"[18] Colonel Rock continued.

Colonel Rock brings up the salient point of this subject. Many precommand courses held throughout the Air Force speak cogently to the formal subject of death and serious injury, particularly regarding the plans and programs available to you as the commander. Many of the courses teach you about the services programs available (including mortuary affairs) or hospital programs (including the many services available at the life skills office). Often overlooked are the details of how the commander should act and what informal actions to take when faced with an uncomfortable situation.

During one such incident, I was on the flight line directing actions during an exercise before our scheduled Operational Readiness Inspection evaluation the following week. Everything had to be perfect. Airplanes were taking off and landing; bombs were being hurriedly loaded; aircrews, specialists, and maintainers were running about—and my cell phone rang. Our squadron's first sergeant informed me that one of our airmen had just found his two-month-old daughter dead in her crib.

This was my first death situation as a squadron commander, and, as such, I didn't have any experience to fall back on. My Shirt mentioned that a similar incident happened months earlier in our wing's transportation squadron. Should I call the transportation squadron commander for some advice? I did, and his counsel made all the difference. Once again, going to a fellow commander for advice always works.

I immediately transferred command of the exercise to my director of operations, and I asked the Shirt, on-duty chaplain, family support center director, and a friend of the airman's family to meet in my office immediately. There, we built a plan of attack to take care of the myriad details that surround a death. Once I was comfortable with the plan, each person handled the areas of his or her particular responsibility. I called my boss to keep him informed and headed to the local hospital where the baby and the family were transported.

Many of the commanders I spoke with who had this experience all agreed that they weren't the most prepared person nor very comfortable with hospitals, chaplains, crying, and things naturally associated with such a terrible incident. Nor was I, but it is something you have to face when the time comes. You *cannot* delegate this responsibility.

I was ushered into the hospital's grieving room, a small, comfortable room with two couches, a couple of lounge chairs, and many tissues. Most hospitals have such an arrangement, and, as was advised in chapter one, you should take the time early in your command to drive to your nearest hospital and look around. Better to do this at your leisure on a sunny Saturday afternoon than in a rush at 0200 on a snowy Thursday morning. I had done so, and it paid off several times over.

What did I do? Probably the same thing you would have done in the same situation. I hugged the parents, I cried with the family, and I let them talk. I listened for a long time. And then, I listened some more. The air was thick with emotion. At first, I was unsure if my presence would be welcomed, particularly in such a grievous situation. My first sergeant assured me it was exactly the right thing to do, and it was.

Next came the need for a memorial service. This particular family was very popular and had many friends and well wishers attending the service. Even though we were right in the middle of a four-day exercise, I arranged for a memorial service. We were particularly fortunate to have a sympathetic group commander and an accommodating wing inspector general who made appropriate changes to the exercise schedule to allow a 60-minute uninterrupted service. I changed out of my chemical gear into a service dress uniform and penned some remarks for use at the memorial service. Our squadron spouses' group, leadership, family, and friends had a wonderful service. The memorial went well, the family was taken care of, and we all got back to our exercise (see "When to Let It Go" in this section).

One commander was called in the middle of a weekday afternoon with news that a teenaged son of one of his SNCOs had a near-death reaction to a drug overdose. He rushed to the hospital with his first sergeant and found the family crowded around their son in the emergency room. It was a terrible sight and one that was uncomfortable for him. Was he in the way? Did they want to see their commander under such personal conditions? The answer was an emphatic "Yes!"

What did he do? How did he react to the unfortunate situation? Again, he did what he thought was the right thing to do and that was to lend his support. He held the hand of the spouse and told the husband (one of his SNCOs) that effective immediately, he was on leave. Not literal leave, of course, but the squadron commander wanted the family to know that the squadron was with them in their time of crisis and that the military member should not come back to work until he got his family situation under control. He was to keep in touch with the first sergeant and was assured the unit would take care of things. The Air Force has a number of excellent programs for situations like these, and the first sergeant was the conduit to helping the family in every way possible.

Although many of the actions taken during the death of a member's spouse or child are the same, there are a few more actions required when the death involves an active duty member. A whole series of processes are set in motion. The Mobility

Support Squadron administers the casualty notification and survivor benefits programs, and the Services Squadron is responsible for mortuary affairs. If the deceased was a service member who died in an accident, there will be a safety investigation run by the wing safety office. There may be media interest, in which case, your wing's public affairs office will be involved. Above all, the squadron naturally will want to look out for the personal needs of the immediate or extended family. All these things are occurring simultaneously, and someone has to be the focal point for coordinating actions and ensuring success—that person is the squadron commander.

Lt Col Matthew Black took the time early in his command tour to plan for such an unfortunate occurrence by writing out a checklist to help him focus on those actions necessary in times of crisis. "I visited Mortuary Affairs and the folks at the Family Support Center to see what programs they had available in such an instance. I was happily amazed to see that they had a great deal of programs available, which I quickly added to my checklist. Fortunately, I never had to use it,"[19] he remembered.

Lt Col Leonard Patrick wasn't as fortunate. He dealt with several deaths during his watch as commander of the 12th Civil Engineering Squadron, Randolph AFB, Texas. One such case involved the off-duty, off-base murder of one of his NCOs. "I received a late evening phone call from the local police department. The first sergeant and I got real busy, real fast," he said. "One of the smartest things we did very early in the process was to assign one of my sharpest young officers as the Summary Courts Officer (SCO). I cleaned everything else off his plate and had him work full time on taking care of the many issues involving the grief-stricken family."[20] The SCO was responsible for arranging flight transportation for those extended family members flying in for the memorial service, ensuring appropriate Serviceman's Government Life Insurance (SGLI) payments were made to the spouse, arranging for full military honors for the funeral, and taking care of the myriad other details involved with such an incident. Colonel Patrick's advice is sound. Depending on your particular situation, consider tasking another squadron member to take sole care of the family's personal needs (billeting reservations, drivers, escorts, child care, yard work) to allow the SCO to focus on the formal service's needs.

Aircraft Accidents

For those who command a flying squadron, one of the worst things is to get a phone call alerting you that one of your aircraft has gone down. Thousands of thoughts naturally will run through your mind—none of them good. Did the pilot and aircrew get out safely? Was anyone hurt on the ground from falling debris? Where is the family? All are significant questions and ones that need to be answered as soon as possible but not before you take the leadership steps necessary to take control of the situation.

There are too many possible scenarios to discuss in any kind of detail here, so this section will rely on the real-life situations of those interviewed who have experienced such a tragedy. What did they do about it?

Lt Col Dennis Jones commanded the 551st Special Operations Squadron (MH-53), a student-training unit located at Kirtland AFB, New Mexico, when he got the call. An MH-53 helicopter was on a routine training mission when in the course of practicing autorotations, the helicopter's tail rotor hit the ground. Normally, this is a bad thing, but in this instance, it rapidly got worse. When the tail rotor struck the ground, debris flew forward into the cabin striking the student pilot in the head. The injury was devastating but not fatal.

After meeting the injured officer on the helipad and seeing him to the ambulance with the rescue personnel, Colonel Jones used his unit's operations desk as a makeshift command post to coordinate those actions necessary outside the base fire and rescue service responsibilities. He knew that people would be calling for information once the word spread quickly that there had been a serious accident that they would want a central number to control the flow of information. Colonel Jones' priorities were clear: the family had to be notified quickly (and personally) before they heard word through a possible unqualified source. As his student pilot was being transported downtown to the local trauma center, he notified the spouse, offering to drive her to the hospital.

The student's spouse obviously was distraught, and he took it upon himself to console her as much as possible while they waited for the news from the emergency surgery team. His goal was to ensure the family had every bit of support it needed inside and outside Air Force channels. In doing so, he enlisted the full-time support of his squadron's assigned flight surgeon, who not only acted as a medical interpreter for the family but also acted as an exceptional calming influence. They both, along with a number of friends of the family, spent the night in the hospital with the pilot's spouse. Fortunately, after many hours of surgery, the officer was alive but not well. He would receive many months of rehabilitation.

Knowing this was going to be a long-term situation, Colonel Jones took the lead in energizing his squadron members to take care of the family and their needs. He set up a baby-sitting schedule for the officer's young children. He energized the squadron's student spouses' group to ensure that round-the-clock coverage of breakfast, lunch, and dinner needs were being met. He ensured invitational orders were written for the student's parents. "When things go bad, the Air Force really bands together as a team. My biggest problem was trying to slow everyone down from trying to help in any way they could and duplicating effort. In the worst of times, it was a tremendous event," Colonel Jones said, "and the Air Force family did an overall outstanding job."[21]

When to Let It Go

The subject of when is it appropriate to stop the grieving process and move on is one that is very personal to you and the squadron and is one that may have different answers. Those commanders who had the unfortunate situation happen to them offer some insights to their experiences.

How did Colonel Jones handle the squadron's flight schedule? Did he ground the helos and stop training for a while? Did he keep the schedule running? Although you may get advice from your group or wing commander, the ultimate decision rests in the lap of the squadron commander. He said, "I shut the squadron down for one day after the accident to allow the squadron to take a breather over what had happened. I didn't want people flying knowing they were thinking about this near-death experience when they should be concentrating on flight training. Similarly, I didn't want everyone to languish over the situation indefinitely. I thought a 24-hour breather was the right thing to do—and it was."[22]

When is it time to stop the grieving process and move on with normal squadron duties? When is it time to let it go? Colonel Patrick said, "Each incident of mine was handled differently. I had to feel the pulse of the squadron to make that determination. In all cases, however, I stopped talking about the incident about a month after the deaths. Everyone in the squadron will have a different grieving process, but they're looking to the commander for his reaction—his words, his mannerisms, and his actions."[23]

The overall advice was this: take 24–48 hours to cease operations (as best as allowable) for your personnel to grieve and reflect on the situation and then get back to work. Although this may look callous and seem insensitive, fear not. The squadron is looking to you for clear guidance and leadership, and they'll recognize the fact that life must go on.

Notes

1. Army Field Manual (FM) 22-100, *Army Leadership*, 31 August 1999.

2. Lt Col Matthew Black, interviewed by author, Maxwell Air Force Base (AFB), Ala., 15 November 2001.

3. Lt Col Lori Montgomery, interviewed by author, Maxwell AFB, Ala., 30 November 2001.

4. Lt Col Kurt Klausner, interviewed by author, Maxwell AFB, Ala., 31 August 2001.

5. Ibid.

6. Black interview.

7. Lt Col Anthony Rock, interviewed by the author, Montgomery, Ala., 14 November 2001.

8. SMSgt Walter Lilley Jr., interviewed by author, Maxwell AFB, Ala., 18 September 2001.

9. Montgomery interview.

10. FM 22-100.

11. Lt Col Dennis Jones, interviewed by author, Maxwell AFB, Ala., 21 November 2001.

12. SMSgt Phil Topper, interviewed by author, Maxwell AFB, Ala., 8 February 2002.

13. FM 22-100.

14. Lilley interview.

15. SMSgt Robert Hill, telephone interview with author, Ellsworth AFB, S.Dak., 22 January 2002.

16. Maj Jay Carroll, interviewed by author, Maxwell AFB, Ala., 14 February 2002.

17. Lt Col Leonard Coleman, interviewed by author, Maxwell AFB, Ala., 30 August 2001.

18. Rock interview.

19. Black interview.

20. Lt Col Leonard Patrick, interviewed by author, Maxwell AFB, Ala., 24 February 2002.

21. Jones interview.

22. Ibid.

23. Patrick, 14 March 2002.

Chapter 6

Cats and Dogs

Although this chapter deals with issues that do not affect every squadron, it does address many issues that do. Some of the issuses are pleasant ones, others are not so pleasant.

Honorary Squadron Commander Programs

Many squadrons have a program in which a prominent member of the local community, often a member of the local government Military Affairs Committee, volunteers and agrees to be your honorary squadron commander. If you're fortunate enough to have one, you're lucky. If your wing does not have such a program, suggest one. If tackled properly, it can be a rewarding experience for both of you.

"Our wing had a very special relationship with the surrounding civilian community," said Lt Col Terry Kono. "And as such, we had a very strong honorary squadron commander program. Although my honorary had a very busy schedule, we made a point of meeting for lunch or talking on the phone or attending wing functions from time to time. I think he was a superb voice to the civilian community about the Air Force mission in general because he knew the squadron so well."[1]

It is probable that your honorary squadron commander will have a specific interest in the professional activities of your squadron, likely because the individual's local employment will closely mirror your unit's mission. For example, the local bank president often will be paired up with the commander of the comptroller squadron, the manager of the local petroleum company might be paired up with the supply squadron commander, or the community police chief will be the "honorary" for the Security Forces Squadron. This common association can be of great benefit to you and your squadron both personally and professionally.

The role the honorary plays is completely up to you and the individual, who can and will be as active in your squadron as you both choose. Common events the honorary should be invited to include all squadron common parties, such as your unit's summer picnic and winter holiday party. If the honorary has small children, extend an invitation to your squadron's children's spring party or May Day get-together. And, don't forget the change of command ceremony—the honorary should be on the secretary's list of distinguished visitors. In most wings, the director of staff handles this program in conjunction with the protocol office.

Closing Down a Squadron

You may be the unfortunate commander who will be your squadron's last one due to an impending closure of your unit. With today's efforts to slim down force structure and realign some Air Force wings and squadrons, it's possible that you'll get caught up in the change, and it might come as a big surprise.

"The news came as a bolt out of the blue," said Lt Col Matthew Black. "I was already behind the power curve because the announced date of closure was almost immediate. It caused great alarm for the personnel in my squadron. Everyone wanted to know where they were going to be assigned, when they had to move, etc. It caught me quite by surprise."[2]

Personnel issues likely will occupy the vast majority of your time. Your major command and numbered air force, as appropriate, will offer some direction. The Air Force Personnel Center also will be heavily involved, and your attention to these major matters will need your complete oversight. Consider asking the AFPC assignment officer(s) to come to your unit to brief your personnel en masse. Arrange for your wing's Mission Support Squadron personnel to attend to help answer any related questions. Planning ahead and paying attention to detail will help avert trouble down the road.

Lt Col Al Hunt was in command of the 13th Airlift Squadron (C-141) at McGuire AFB, New Jersey, when he was told his squadron was to be deactivated. He offers this advice: "Although there's not a lot of stuff out there telling you how to close a squadron, don't reinvent the wheel. Find someone

158

who's already had that experience and pick the person's brain. Call the USAF Historical Society (located at Maxwell AFB, Alabama) for advice and direction. They were a good source of information regarding the heraldry of my unit."[3]

This is a time for a commander to be a leader. If rumors are flying around, try to stop them. You can do so by having an out-of-cycle commander's call, for example, to address the unit's concerns. Arm yourself with as many facts as you can and talk to your troops directly—face to face. They will be thirsty for your leadership and frankness. Tell them not to panic and assure them that they won't "get lost in the dust" of the reorganization. Many of your unit personnel will get absorbed in other wing units, but some will undoubtedly have to move off station. Short-notice permanent change of station actions are inevitable in these situations and will have to be treated accordingly. Your days will be long.

Lt Col Wilfred Cassidy has faced this situation of retiring the squadron colors twice during his Air Force career. He said, "One of my greatest challenges was keeping the squadron's personnel motivated. I had to constantly remind them of how important they were to the wing's mission, and the fact that our squadron was closing did not mean they were any less important."[4]

Once the formal actions are taken care of and are under way, now is the time to relax. Have a celebration! Find an energetic squadron member (or 10) and have them organize a going-away party for the entire squadron. Those commanders who have faced this situation all remarked that it was the exact thing to do at the end of such a tumultuous period. They held a huge party. They invited the wing staff. They invited all former squadron commanders and those former squadron members who still lived in the local area. Some designed T-shirts signifying the event and captured it on cotton. Others designed a "shutdown" coin for everyone. "We even invited our MAJCOM functionals. We had it professionally videotaped as going-away souvenirs for the squadron personnel. Although no one wanted the 13th Airlift Squadron to close, we made the best of a bad situation. It was a class act,"[5] said Lt Col Alan Hunt. Whatever you choose, make it big!

Money Management

There are two facets to money management: funds associated with your annual budget (as provided by your wing through the comptroller) and those funds that fall within your squadron (in the form of snack bars, fund-raisers, and so on). You undoubtedly will attend a MAJCOM precommand course before your assumption of command. Here, you will learn the major rules of squadron finance and what you can and cannot legally or ethically spend money on. I won't attempt to tackle the fundamental issues here, but I do want to give you some good advice: Pay attention! Without question, the issue of money management can be your fastest ticket to trouble— serious trouble—if either pot of money is mismanaged. Spend considerable time studying this area.

Money management at the squadron level is something you probably haven't had to worry about. Before, if you needed new toner for your printer, you may have asked to use the squadron International Merchant Purchase Authorization Card to buy it without regard for the checkbook balance. Need a new pair of boots? Just ask your mobility shop or resource advisor for a pair (with heretofore no regard for the financial bottom line). As commander, you are now responsible for every dime your squadron makes or spends.

"I spent our allotted funds as if they were my own money," said Colonel Kono. "You always have a need for more money, so it's incredibly important to prioritize a limited budget. I know it sounds like micromanagement, but I wanted to be aware of every dime that was being spent. We had short-term management—30/60/90-day looks; I kept an eye on the annual budget, but with an eye toward inflation rather than just the previous year's spend plan; a detailed priority list for the end-of-year spend out, if money dropped from our MAJCOM; and a five-year look ahead to account for wear and tear on equipment. I made sure the squadron as a whole understood how we spent the money."[6]

I hope that you will have an NCO in your squadron who is designated as your squadron resource advisor (RA). If not, get one. Assign the role as an additional duty and send the person to the necessary training. Some wings have a formal training

160

session conducted by the wing's comptroller squadron, and others have a less formal training program through the group RA. It is your RA who is primarily responsible for the day-to-day activities of your checkbook, but never forget that it's *your* checkbook. If your resource advisor makes or allows an unethical, illegal purchase using government funds, you and you alone must bear the full responsibility for such actions.

For example, although my squadron had a very large budget, and even given that I was fortunate to have a smart and experienced resource advisor, it was my policy to be informed of any purchase (outside what we had already established as norms) over $1,500. If something didn't pass my commonsense cross-check, I'd be sure to ask repeatedly if what we were about to purchase was legal and ethical. The word quickly got around that this was high on my list of priorities. The size of your squadron and unit budget will determine what your policy will be, but I strongly suggest that you get hold of your squadron purse strings as soon as possible, and never, never let that checkbook get out of your sight or control. If you do, you will do so at your own peril.

Lt Col Jay Carlson was not only concerned about the financial plan of his own squadron but was concerned about the financial plans of every squadron—and the wing—due to his duties as the 18th Wing's Contracting Squadron commander. He offers this advice: "It's critical for the squadron commander to fully grasp the responsibilities of having a viable spend plan, listed in order of priority, well before you approach the end of the fiscal year. You should also check with your group commander to determine what his or her priorities for your money are as well. It's not unusual for any unspent squadron dollars to roll into group and wing buckets. Essentially, if you don't spend it smartly, someone else will!"[7]

Another area that was likely covered in your MAJCOM commander's course is that of funds generated from your squadron's snack bars and fund-raisers—different animals entirely. There is an upper limit on how much money you can have in any one fund at any one time, and given the size of your unit, it is something that is potentially ripe with mismanagement—abuse that can get you into trouble easily. Have a standard, announce it to all, and publish it on every squadron bulletin board.

One thing is certain—squadron command can be personally expensive. Some commanders took it in stride by saying that squadron command was a once-in-a-lifetime event, and they knew to budget for the increased out-of-pocket expenses. Others aggressively worked with their unit's booster club to set policies for unit's unfunded purchases. Who should pay for flowers in the event of a death in the family—you, the troop's section, the squadron Top 3, or the booster club? Some squadrons have a program that congratulates the parents of a newborn child with a care package that includes a month's worth of diapers, food, formula, and a stuffed toy. This is certainly a great idea for the young airman who can use the free baby goods, but who is going to pay for it? All these events need some thought before they happen. You'll hopefully have some thoughtful personnel who come up with great ideas to help others (which is a good boost for squadron morale), but it is your responsibility to follow up with the all-important—and often overlooked—details.

Dorm Inspections

Dorm inspections are an integral part of a commander's job; but you, the commander, can add impact to the routine. You'll likely have at least some members of your squadron living in the base's government dormitories. Get your first sergeant's feelings on the matter, but participate in dorm room inspections. How often you accompany the first sergeant or how many rooms you inspect at any one time will be entirely up to you. Dorm life can be a source of many disciplinary issues for your young airmen, so understanding how and where they live will give you a better insight into their lives.

Consider these techniques. When you do participate in dorm room inspections, leave something in the room to let the airman know you were personally there. Some commanders left troops a note of congratulations (when things looked good), an attaboy note to say how proud you are of their attention to detail. "Five good inspections in a row earned them a 24-hour pass and public recognition," said one commander. Maj Jay Carroll put clean and organized dorm rooms high on his list of priorities: "I gave a 72-hour pass every month to the airman who ha[d] the most improved dorm room. What an instant success! One thing that energizes young people most is the reward of having time off. I went from a terrible dorm room problem to no problem at all."[8] Another commander left troops a lollipop or other piece of candy on their desks to let them know he cared enough to personally inspect their rooms and enforce a common standard. Additionally, I arranged for several of my junior officers to follow my first sergeant and me on our rounds of the dorms. I thought it was important for their professional officer development and was another tool of experience in their toolbox to use when they get the opportunity to command.

Conversely, if you witness a room that is clearly out of standards, let the troop know this as well but not with a note. This needs to be handled face to face. Confer with your first sergeant to determine the best course of action. Let the airman know directly that living in a government housing facility is a privilege, not a right, and a privilege that can be taken away if the situation isn't corrected immediately. One commander handled it this way: after a failed inspection, he had the dorm room occupant and the individual's supervisor meet him or the first sergeant at 0600 on the following Saturday morning for a full and complete reinspection. Believe me, the situation will likely get resolved immediately and, hopefully, will not return.

If you see an area in the dorms that you believe requires serious attention—and serious money—such as the need for a new recreation room television, necessary upgrades to community kitchens, or renovations to public restrooms, consider inviting your group commander for an inspection or two. It may have been some time since he or she conducted dorm inspections; taking this opportunity will give your airmen the attention they deserve. After all, the dorm is home to them, the place they go after eight to 12 hours or more of hard work. With O-6 attention comes O-6 concern. And, the group commander can vie for the necessary funding to purchase any needed furnishing upgrades.

Most wings have a policy of keeping the dormitories filled to near-100 percent capacity. Until this magic number is exceeded with younger, newer airmen, those older airmen (and perhaps E-4s as well) will not have the option of moving out. This naturally results in several unmarried residents being unhappy with mandatory dorm placement. Generally, the wing's Support Group commander, acting in the capacity of the installation commander (while in some wings this responsibility falls under the wing commander), will have well-established and published policies regarding dorm facility management. Check with that office soon to find out what the exact policies are, because you will not be in command long before one of your airmen asks to get out of the dorm.

Regardless of the specific policies at your base, many airmen will do what is called "ghosting." This is where several airmen will get together, pool their money, and live out of an apartment or house downtown in the local community. Because they are required to live in the dormitory, their housing allowance is still taken from their paychecks because of their government housing status. In effect, they're living on their own and out of their pockets. You'll first notice this when you conduct a dorm room inspection to find virtually nothing in the room. I was alarmed when I first witnessed this but soon came to realize that ghosting is not illegal and is often allowed by the squadron commander (as long as the airman's financial obligations off base are faithfully met). I allowed it and never had a problem.

US Government Travel Card

Here's another area that may prove painful for you and your first sergeant and, certainly one that definitely needs your personal attention. If not handled up front with a personal policy letter from you, it will crop up later when the government-issued credit card is inappropriately used. Enough commanders raised this issue during interviews to include it in this section.

By regulation, every member of your unit will be issued a government credit card for use during professional travel and related services. Again, your MAJCOM squadron commander's course should cover the proper and legal uses of the card. Unfortunately, many command-sponsored courses don't offer advice on how to manage your program.

Although your young airmen may be the worst offenders with the card, misuse is by no means limited to that target group. It is necessary to have a published letter from you that requires their personal signature, explaining in clear and unambiguous detail the appropriate uses of the credit card. Because this problem is not new, you may have inherited an acceptable policy from your predecessor.

The vast majority of the problems come from unit personnel who get caught in a fiscal bind and end up using the government cards for personal use "to get through this bad financial period." What many of them do not understand is that you, as the commander (or your personally designated credit card administrator), get a monthly financial statement from the credit card company listing every transaction on each card of your personnel, highlighting those offenders who have failed to pay off their accounts within a 30-, 60-, or 90-day period. A quick scan of the report can help you spot misuse. Use of the government credit card to pay off other personal debts is also common and can easily be spotted each month. A local transaction at "Big Al's TV Repair" should be a certain tip-off.

Every commander interviewed for this book had a written policy in effect. Many of the commanders interviewed had unique ways of controlling the card's use (and potential misuse). For example, one commander of a very large squadron was responsible for a sizable group of young airmen. She had a straightforward approach to preventing potential misuse—she confiscated all cards for E-3s and below and handed them out, through the first sergeant, to those who were ordered to temporary duty. She commented that very few personnel were offended by this seemingly harsh approach, and many more were grateful to be relieved of the burden of having to carry it around. Obviously, this approach works best for a squadron that rarely deploys and can be an administrative nightmare to those who travel often.

Notes

1. Lt Col Terry Kono, telephone interview with author, Dyess Air Force Base (AFB), Tex., 20 December 2001.

2. Lt Col Matthew Black, interviewed by author, Maxwell AFB, Ala., 15 November 2001.

3. Lt Col Alan Hunt, interviewed by author, Maxwell AFB, Ala., 20 September 2001.

4. Lt Col Wilfred Cassidy, interviewed by author, Maxwell AFB, Ala., 25 March 2002.

5. Hunt interview.

6. Kono interview.

7. Lt Col Jay Carlson, interviewed by author, Maxwell AFB, Ala., 27 February 2002.

8. Maj Jay Carroll, interviewed by author, Maxwell AFB, Ala., 16 February 2002.

Chapter 7

Your Exit Strategy

Unlike the method by which you were notified of assuming command, your departure from the top job likely will be much less subtle. Current Air Force policy dictates that the standard tour of command be pegged at a full 24 months, although many times this is not the case.

Finishing the Job and Leaving in Style

In most instances, you will have the luxury of planning your successor's change of command ceremony, and preparing the squadron for your departure, as well as your successor's arrival. If you've commanded in style, you'll certainly want to leave in style.

Time Compression

Regardless of how much time you have between the notification and your actual relinquishing of command, it never seems to be enough. You are constantly rushed. Time is always compressed at the end of a command tour because of the flood of events and requirements that engulf the outgoing commander. Performance reports need to be closed out (officer, enlisted, and civilian appraisals), major squadron projects need to be completed, disciplinary problems should be resolved, and people should be thanked for their support—this list could go on and on.

After reviewing the situation, the outgoing commander normally concludes there simply is not enough time to complete everything, and it's best to organize and prioritize actions. One former commander explained how he broke these actions down into three helpful categories describes as follows:

Critical Tasks. Those items that need to be completed by the outgoing commander before the change of command—for one reason or another, the incoming commander cannot (or should not) accomplish these items.

Proverb for Leadership

Weak leaders who have not trained their subordinates sometimes say, "My organization can't do without me." Many people, used to being at the center of the action, begin to feel as if they're indispensable. You've heard them, "I can't take a day off. I have to be there all the time. I must watch my subordinate's every move, or who knows what will happen?" But no one is irreplaceable. The Air Force is not going to stop functioning because one leader—no matter how senior or central—steps aside.[1]

Necessary Tasks. Items that the outgoing commander should complete before the changeover. The incoming commander could possibly accomplish these items, but the outgoing commander is much better suited to finish the task.

Nice-to-Do Tasks. Items that the outgoing commander possibly would like to accomplish before leaving. The new commander also may be able to accomplish these tasks easily.

The following examples describe various types of tasks that you, as the outgoing commander, may be faced with before turning the unit flag over to your successor.

Critical tasks normally center around the squadron's mission and people. The first action is for *you* to tell your people of the upcoming change of command. Many commanders hit the nail on the head by calling a special meeting of all available unit supervisors, telling them the news, and asking them to spread the word quickly. They wanted their personnel to hear the news from within the squadron instead of through the rumor mill or from someone outside the squadron.

Another critical task is the completion of performance reports. I hope that you've planned ahead and are not staring at a flood of reports—all being generated simultaneously because you are leaving. You will always have some reports to accomplish, and they deserve the same careful work that all others received; don't shortchange the troops being rated, however, because you have a short suspense!

One commander who was caught on a short-notice assignment (to another good job) requested extra time to complete the necessary performance reports. He needed to be forceful with his arguments, and he finally convinced the bureaucracy, up through major command personnel, that he needed the extension to write a large number of important reports accurately and effectively.

Most commanders consider turning over a fully up and running unit to their successor a critical task. Aim to finish all performance reports, decoration packages, personnel paperwork, and post-inspection reports possible before the change of command.

Regarding discipline, four former commanders specifically emphasized clearing up all discipline and UCMJ matters before the change of command. They considered this task essential. Nobody wants to inherit problems, and the commander who initiated the disciplinary action is in by far the best position to complete the action in a consistent, just manner. One commander inherited a serious disciplinary problem when he took over his unit. He had difficulty completing the action effectively because the case involved a long history of circumstances that he never could fully ascertain. He was determined not to hand over any such problems to his successor.

Reality is often such that cleaning up all matters involving UCMJ actions before your departure is simply not possible due to the length of investigation or litigation. There may have been an incident on the eve of your change of command that cannot be closed out as fast. When you must pass on such an issue, make sure you spend time with your successor to discuss the matter thoroughly. Your first sergeant will be schooled in these matters and will be able to guide the new commander through the legal paperwork necessary in switching responsibility from you to your successor.

Finally, and most important, one commander said that during his last week, he went around the squadron to every shift—day and night—thanking each member for the member's hard work and support. Thanking each member of your unit individually may be impossible and fall under the nice-to-do category, but in some way, thanking your people for their support is critical. Here, a final commander's call may be a viable tool for closure.

I have listed below a few items I'd classify as necessary.

1. With regard to the unit's mission, as commander, ensure any updates to unit procedures or policies are completed. If your operations officer, deputy commander, supervisor, or superintendent is not departing the squadron with you, the mission is usually not a problem. They will provide mission continuity during the transition of commanders, so the daily operation should continue smoothly unless there are unusual circumstances in progress, such as a major revision of the mission.

2. Regarding people, if possible, at some point before the change of command, stop all personnel moves inside the squadron. The new commander will be in charge for the next two years or so and deserves the right to make some of these decisions. One commander who was being replaced by his operations officer let his successor make most of these decisions during the last six weeks before the changeover. He reasoned that the new commander would have to live with the decisions.

3. Any awards and decorations packages should be completed before the change of command. As the outgoing commander, you are in a much better position to judge the accuracy of these packages than your successor. Also, if you are departing the base, you may get involved in your own nomination package.

4. If it is at all possible, the outgoing and incoming commanders need to get together and discuss the state of the unit—a necessary task. Most outgoing commanders will initiate the process by calling the new commander and offering their congratulations and any desired assistance.

5. If you are staying on base in another capacity, offer your counsel any time the new commander has a question, but give assurances that you will mind your own business after the change of command. Don't forget your spouse. It's a good idea for your spouses to get together as well.

Remember, you're still the commander until you pass the flag. A couple of former commanders related how they had to hold back their replacements who were a little too anxious to get in the middle of squadron business before officially taking over. A few commanders told me they invited the next commander to the squadron for discussions only after duty hours to avoid placing their people in an awkward position with regard to loyalty. Other commanders related that they personally escorted their successors around their squadrons, introducing the unit members. Safe advice here is to handle the matter in whatever way is natural for you and the squadron.

Because many squadrons change command during the summer months, one item that seems to escape most commanders is the importance of your squadron's financial plan for the next fiscal year. In addition, this is one area sure to be out of sight of the incoming commander who will have many items to handle in the new job. Lt Col Jay Carlson offers this advice: "With many commands changing out during late summer or early fall, there will only be three months or so before the end of the fiscal year when you'll need to have a detailed financial plan ready for wing review. It would be a great idea for you to pass on the logic behind your end-of-year financial game plan to your successor. Understanding that his or her priorities may be different than yours, at least he'll have an educated plan to work from."[2] Great advice to help the officer who follows you in command.

For miscellaneous paperwork, I recommend that you complete as many paperwork actions as possible. Most paperwork will fall into the necessary category, but you should decide what is critical, necessary, or nice to do. Numerous commanders said they worked hard to leave an empty in-box for the next commander.

Many items can fall into the nice-to-do category. It would be nice to have a final commander's call, a "finis" flight, a final temporary duty or deployment with the unit, a final dinner with your squadron's supervisors, and so on. As outgoing commander, you know best how much time you have and how your priorities stack up—your decisions all the way.

Going Out in Style

The squadron likely will want to throw you a farewell party, and their spouses may want to do something for your spouse also. Anything goes here. Your, and their, call. The only suggestion I offer is to have the functions before the change of command, not after it when you are no longer the commander. Some commanders did this, and they all chalked it up as a failure.

Change of Command Ceremony

Don't forget, this is your successor's big day—not yours. Normally, the outgoing commander and squadron plan the change of command ceremony. Each wing usually has a set way of holding these affairs. Certainly, follow the wing commander's guidelines, but go ahead and add your personal touch to the affair, something different. Go out in style! (Just remember, the change of command is the incoming commander's day in the sun and a once-in-a-lifetime experience—honor that.) Don't feel restricted to having the ceremony in a hangar or at the club. Some commanders showed quite a bit of variety. One commander had his changeover outside by the base's new static display aircraft and the reception in the newly remodeled base museum, a first for both ideas.

As you plan, consider doing as one commander with whom I discussed this subject did in placing an emphasis on nailing down the many details early. This will require a project officer or sharp noncommissioned officer. You may want to pick two—someone with experience and someone who deserves some limelight but maybe doesn't have the experience. Challenge them to make the ceremony one the unit will be proud of and one the wing and the incoming commander will remember.

Proverb for Command

Commanders with personal courage realize their subordinate leaders need room to work and grow. This
doesn't mean you let your folks make the same mistakes repeatedly. Part of your responsibility as a
leader is to help ensure your subordinates succeed.
You can achieve this through empowering and coach-
ing. Train your subordinates to plan, prepare, execute,
and assess well enough to operate independently.
Provide sufficient purpose, direction, and motivation
for them to operate in support of the overall plan.[3]

Consider your final speech to the unit. Usually, after the actual change of command, the outgoing and incoming commanders are asked to say a few words to the audience. If your
emotions haven't gotten the best of you yet, they've got one
more chance, and the odds are that they'll get you now. Most
former commanders recommended that you keep your speech
short and sweet, concentrating on thanking the many people
who supported you during your tenure as squadron commander.

In the days following the ceremony, stay away from the
squadron—give the new commander room to operate. Take
some leave, if possible. Some of the commanders interviewed
told me they never went back to their old units; others related
they waited a couple of months; still others told me they had
to go back to attend to business fairly soon after the ceremony
but made their stay as short as possible. Lt Col Roderick Zastrow agreed with all three strategies. He said, "It's important
to exit quietly. I found it important to discreetly depart the
change of command location and only involve myself in unit
matters when follow-up, if any, was required. Likewise, once
departed, stay departed. As you might like as well, don't give
the appearance of checking up on the squadron by bugging the

173

new commander or old cronies left behind. Little can undermine your successor's credibility more than rumors of or actual unsolicited ex-commander follow-up."[4]

One final topic: Perhaps the most important people in your life cannot be neglected—your family. Your family undoubtedly made countless sacrifices during your tenure in command, and deserve as much, if not more, recognition and thanks than you do. Recognize them in your speech, thank them privately after the ceremony, and enjoy their time as much as you can.

The best job you'll ever have in the United States Air Force is now behind you.

Notes

1. Army Field Manual (FM) 22-100, *Army Leadership*, 31 August 1999.
2. Lt Col Jay Carlson, interviewed by author, Maxwell Air Force Base, (AFB) Ala., 27 February 2002.
3. FM 22-100.
4. Lt Col Roderick Zastrow, interviewed by author, Maxwell AFB, Ala., 3 May 2002.

Glossary

AAC	Airman's Advisory Council
AB	Air Base
ASBC	Air and Space Basic Course
AFB	Air Force Base
ACC	Air Combat Command
AFPC	Air Force Personnel Center
AFSC	Air Force Specialty Code
ALS	Airman Leadership School
APZ	above the promotion zone
AWACS	Airborne Warning and Control System
BDU	battle dress uniform
CCAF	Community College of the Air Force
CJCS	Chairman of the Joint Chiefs of Staff
CSS	Computer Systems Squadron
DO	Director of Operations
EPR	Enlisted Performance Report
EQUAL	Enlisted Quarterly Assignment Listing
IG	inspector general
IMPAC	International Merchant Purchase Authorization Card
JA	judge advocate
MAJCOM	major command
MEO	Military Equal Opportunity
MPF	Military Personnel Flight
NAF	numbered air force
NATO	North Atlantic Treaty Organization
NCO	noncommissioned officer
OPR	Officer Performance Report
OPSTEMPO	operations tempo
ORI	operations readiness inspection
OSI	Office of Special Investigation
PCS	permanent change of station
PERSTEMPO	personnel tempo
PME	professional military education
PRF	Promotion Recommendation Form
RA	resource advisor
SCO	summary courts officer

SFS	Security Forces Squadron
SMO	strategic mobility
SNCO	senior noncommissioned officer
SOS	Squadron Officer School
TDY	temporary duty
UCA	Unit Climate Assessment
UCMJ	Uniform Code of Military Justice
USAF FSA	United States Air Force First Sergeant Academy